Miriam Bäckström Luisa Lambri Elisa Sighicelli Roy Exley Anne Zahalka Pavel Büchler
Sharon Kivland Jane Rendell David Williams Paul Ryan Sam Taylor-Wood Keren Amiran
Paul Seawright Mark Durden Patricia Macdonald Marzena Pogorzaly James Lawson
Garry Fabian Miller Peter Finnemore Jem Southam David Chandler Susanne Ramsenthaler
Susanna Beaumont Stella Santacatterina David Alan Mellor John Riddy Simon Morrissey

Anne Zalhalka *Fortresses and Frontiers, Untitled No. 1A*, 1993

portfolio

the catalogue of contemporary
photography in britain

introduction

The new look of this issue takes account of a survey which we conducted earlier this year in which readers were asked how they would like to see the magazine being developed. While a large number responded that it should remain the same, in future images and text for each feature will be more closely integrated, resulting in a larger number of colour and duotone reproductions. We will also feature longer thematic essays on specific genres or topics. In this issue Roy Exley has contrasted the work of three European photographers – Miriam Bäckström (Sweden), Luisa Lambri and Elisa Sighicelli (Italy), and we feature a number of artists exhibiting in the UK – Anne Zahalka (Australia), Sharon Kivland, David Williams, Sam-Taylor Wood, Paul Seawright, Patricia Macdonald, Garry Fabian Miller, Jem Southam, Susanne Ramsenthaler, Keren Amiran, Margena Porgorzaly, John Riddy and Peter Finnemore. Thank you to everyone who participated in the survey. For those of you who haven't yet had an opportunity, you'll find a short questionnaire inserted into this issue – if you can find the time to respond, it would be appreciated.

Pat Macdonald from the publication *Once in Europa*, 1999

Anne Zalhalka, *Aqua Golf*, 1998

Miriam Bäckström, *Set Constructions*, 1995-99

Sharon Kivland, *le bonheur des femmes*, 2000

number 31 june 2000

Published in June and December by Portfolio Gallery
Photography Workshop (Edinburgh) Limited
43 Candlemaker Row, Edinburgh EH1 2QB, UK
Tel (44) 0131 220 1911
Fax (44) 0131 226 4287

Email portfolio@ednet.co.uk

subscriptions

United Kingdom
Individuals £30 for 4 issues / £17 for 2 issues
Institutions, Libraries and Colleges £45 for
4 issues / £25 for 2 issues

Europe £45 for 4 issues / £25 for 2 issues

Worldwide Air £55 for 4 issues / £30 for 2 issues

distribution

UK Museum and Gallery Bookshops:
PORTFOLIO, 43 Candlemaker Row
Edinburgh EH1 2QB, UK
Tel (44) 0131 220 1911 Fax (44) 0131 226 4287

retail

Art Data, 12 Bell Industrial Estate
50 Cunnington Street, London W4 5HB
Tel (44) 0181 747 1061
Fax (44) 0181 742 2319

Inside Front Cover Miriam Bäckström, *Estate of a Deceased Person*,
1992-96 *(detail)*, **Courtesy of Nils Stærk**

contents

Luisa Lambri, *Untitled (Absolutely Necessary Series) (detail)*, 1999

Garry Fabian Miller, *Petworth Windows*, 1999

Jem Southam, *River Bride, Burton Bradstock, Dorset*, 1999

Elisa Sighicelli, *Monterey: Armchairs*, 1999

Editor **Gloria Chalmers**

Editorial Assistants **Lesley Young** and **Catherine Williams**

Subscriptions and Sales **Elizabeth Pardoe**

Design Consultants **Tayburn Corporate**

Typesetting **Patricia Bartie**

Set in Foundry Sans **The Foundry**, London

ISSN 1354-4446ISSN 1354-4446

Printed on Consort Royal Satin manufactured by Donside Paper Company, Aberdeen

Reprographics by Leeds Photo Litho

Printed by Speedprint, Leeds

THE SCOTTISH **ARTS** COUNCIL

Funded by **THE ARTS COUNCIL** OF ENGLAND

·EDINBVRGH·
THE CITY OF EDINBURGH COUNCIL

Into the Interior

Three European Photographers: Miriam Bäckström, Luisa Lambri and Elisa Sighicelli

ROY EXLEY

The deserted interior with all its connotations, histories, memories and emotive signals, features at the canonic heart of the work of Miriam Bäckström, Luisa Lambri and Elisa Sighicelli. Each of these artists, however, has her own agenda in focusing on this site whose mythological resonance burrows deep into our collective psyche.

What is home? Well, many things, of course, but the essence of home is the warmth and security of the familiar, the tried and the tested, right through from the intimate human relationships experienced there, to the accrued and personalised material comforts, and the memories of the events that they trigger. The rhythms of our movements from room to room (which Georges Perec famously documented in his essay, 'The Apartment', in his *Species of Spaces*) that map out our daily routines, and even the mechanical rhythms of the automatic kettle or pop-up toaster, energise its spaces, transforming a house into a home. Principally, however, it is the focal site of our lives as they are lived, with all their affirmative and repetitive patterns, their attendant permutations and complications. Take away the life, the human interactions in all their shades, tender, fiery, callous or indifferent, and there remains an empty shell, a faint palimpsest that withers even as you watch.

As soon as we cease to take for granted what we are seeing when we look at a photograph of such a scene, and begin to analyse the visual information that its two-dimensional surface conveys, only then can we start to appreciate the complexities that are lost to the ever-shifting, scanning glance of our everyday vision – re-inventing what our busy lives have demoted to the periphery. In doing so, of course, we rely upon our faith in the indexical veracity of such an image. The same applies to narrative scenes in a film – we trust what we see in order to maintain the fiction, to perpetuate the illusion – where the apparent truth is often no more than a carefully wrought veneer.

The Swedish artist Miriam Bäckström, in her series of photographs, *Set Constructions*, exposes the film-set for what it is, a minefield of deceptions, a Pandora's Box of surprises, whose consequent de-mystification deflates and discredits its claims to the truth. In her documentary-style images, Bäckström blows the cover of film-set constructions by revealing their unfinished edges – the scaffolding, the incomplete ceilings, the false walls and floors that merge seamlessly into trompe l'oeil backdrops – the margins of the veneer whose flimsy deceptions promulgate a whole suite of synthetic truths. Just as any demolished fantasy does, this leaves the viewer in limbo, but at the same time in awe of the effective simplicity with which these fabricated truths are achieved. In taking these photographs, Bäckström often adopts the position of the absent film camera – these images are permeated by a sense of absence – but her stills camera having a different format and with a wider field-of-view, captures and betrays, time after time, the undisguised artifice on the peripheries of these scenes.

In one image from *Set Constructions*, we witness a 1960's executive's living-room replete with all its status-seeking trappings, the panorama window, the Scandinavian teak glass-topped table, long leather sofa, 'feature' stone-clad wall, and oatmeal fitted carpet. So far so good, but before we have time to surmise upon the life-style to go with this scene, our eye wanders to the fringes of the image, and we notice, at the top, the raw, unfinished edge of the false polystyrene ceiling, jutting out over the scene, suspended by cords from some point high up, beyond the frame, in the yawning spaces of a utilitarian industrial building. On the right side of the image, the trendy stone wall comes to an abrupt end, its artifice betrayed by its wafer-thin edge.

If the image of a deserted home conveys an undercurrent of melancholia, it becomes an overwhelming torrent in Bäckström's series of photographs, *Estate of a Deceased Person*, where any imminence, so often a derivative of absence, is totally missing. The person whose slippers are still beside the bed, and whose newspaper still lies on the sofa, is not about to return, to put on those slippers and sit down to catch up with the latest news, for this person is now dead. Bäckström's series of impassive images showing the interiors of houses of people who have recently died seem to be a breach of confidence,

Miriam Bäckström, Set Constructions, 1995-99 *(above)*

Luisa Lambri, Untitled (Absolutely Necessary Series), 1999 *(previous page)*

Miriam Bäckström, Estate of a Deceased Person, 1992-96

opening up the lives of people which are now closed down. The material imprints left by people's lives, that are conserved here, left exactly where they touched those lives, express the painful reality of the finality of death, with its fall-out of unfinished business and unfulfilled pleasures. These images make for uncomfortable viewing, we have no right to be here, to be intruding upon a privacy which can no longer be defended. What is most poignant here, however, is the contrast between these views, and Bäckström's series, *Model homes*, *1998*, where she has photographed the mock-up rooms which are part and parcel of an exhibition of Scandinavian furniture design. Here are depicted fantasies of a perfection which no money can buy, each a tableau of immaculate deception, designed to be construed as that towards which we must aspire, but whose achievement would only be possible if our lives were to be frozen into a series of moments like the photographs themselves. Just as this perfection has never lived, the imperfection of the deceased's homes has, but won't again. Each of these scenes is as transient as the other, but the ones with the cast off traces of peoples lives are the ones which linger in the memory, bringing a lump to the throat.

Just as devoid of life are the photographs of interiors by the Milan-based artist, Luisa Lambri, and Elisa Sighicelli, who is based in London. Luisa Lambri's photographs are the products of intuition and empathy. She visits the iconic buildings of high-profile modernist architects, such as Alvar Aalto, le Corbusier, Louis Kahn, and Ludwig Mies van der Rohe, and enters into a relationship with them. Her images transcend the documentary – despite having a documentary mien – imbuing the objectivity of those places with a pervasive subjectivity. In his last writings in *Aesthetic Theory*, Theodor Adorno brought an exegesis of the decay and dissipation which besets the residual subjectivity in a work of art when it is exposed to public view. This subjectivity is, he argues, rapidly eroded away, dissolved, absorbed and translocated into the surrounding cultural milieu. The aura of empathy, which pervades Lambri's images, seems to compensate for this loss of subjectivity, indeed, restores it through a transfusion of her own subjectivity.

We find, in the taut, personal, and often melancholic images that Lambri creates, a subjugation of the sense of loss that these sites exude, her presence is somehow woven into their fabric. The closer we examine her photographs, the more the traces of her subjective imprint become evident. Lambri orientates herself within these

Luisa Lambri, Untitled (Absolutely Necessary Series), 1999

Elisa Sighicelli, Senza Mondo I, II, III, 1998

spaces in such a way – often evading the tell-tale trade marks of the architect's touch – that she constructs a barely perceptible phantom of her own subjectivity. Lambri's eye penetrates these buildings in such a way that she reads their semiotic rather than their literal meanings, capturing their essence rather than their veneer of identity, their substance rather than their celebrity. To celebrate, or even recognise the work of these architects is not the point here.

In her photographs of Mies van der Rohe's *Tugendhat Villa* in Brno, from her *Absolutely Necessary Series (1999)*, we are confronted with images which are almost abstract in their demeanour, the forms of the numerous vertical and horizontal elements in the window and door-frames – evocative of the rectilinear grids of the paintings of Mondrian or Malevich – take on a new significance in these pensive close-up views, bringing the viewer into a fresh relationship with van der Rohe's architecture. Lambri offers it to us as an extension of herself, these images resonate with her presence. Unlike the work of Bäckström, there is no exposure of artifice here, no penetrations of the surface, but an eerie, sometimes uncanny transformation of these surfaces and spaces into something new, amplifying rather than denying their reality, somehow restoring Adorno's leached away subjectivity, and indeed, that lost aura that Walter Benjamin attributed to the use of photography in his essay, *Art in the Age of Mechanical Reproduction*. Glass, metal, polished stone and exotic veneers, in all their pristine precision dominate the surfaces here, reflecting and relaying the incidental light with a crystalline clarity which is mirrored by the crisply deliberate delineation of these studies.

In an interview with Massimiliano Gioni, Lambri stated, "I see architecture as autobiography, the places photographed as self-portraits. I'm not interested in documenting the architectural qualities of a building". Whereas tourists take snap-shots of places they visit, not only to create memorabilia, but also to furnish evidence of their presence at those sites, Lambri in her poignant photographic studies, stamps her presence on these iconic buildings, leaving us in no doubt as to her intimate relationship with them, as she conveys their cold, stark, but enduring beauty.

Elisa Sighicelli's images are more intimate; the interior spaces depicted in her back-lit C-type prints are rented apartments. We are not sure of their status, as all the clutter of daily living is missing, they are bereft of all the usual signs of occupation, have they been vacated – or is a visit from the mother-in-law is expected? Whatever the case, there is no sign of life, no human presence, a factor which creates a tension in these scenes. These images are haunted by this absence which is more a deferred presence, an imminence. Many of Sighicelli's images convey the feeling that these people, whose surrogates we are, in these spaces, are close at hand – just out of shot or soon to return, or about to move in – they are, nevertheless missing here, missing now.

In the images in her *Senza Mondo* (1998), series – six views of the same apartment – Sighicelli questions what comprises now and how we perceive here, are these merely concepts or is their resolution crucial? These scenarios are, like the photographs themselves, balanced between reality and illusion, whose boundaries are elusive, where are they and how do we perceive them? Enigma creeps in from all sides, bringing a sublime edge to her work.

The viewer experiences no sense of intrusion here, unlike Bäckström's views of homes of the deceased; we feel welcome here, we are simply awaiting the imminent return of the missing ones, whoever they might be. We begin to analyse their traces, the trappings and furnishings, but few clues are offered in these dimly lit scenes, where the shaft of light slicing through a half open window, could be from another universe. Partially lit, the objects in the room become disjointed, fragmentary, their silhouettes becoming mere noumena in the penumbral ambiguity. Caught between shadow and highlight, in a scene snatched from some film noir classic, identities are obscured and the sense of enigma is amplified. No insights here, our analyses amounting to nought. The colours are muted and cluster around burnt umber, fomenting a dour atmosphere, adding to the sense of loss which hovers in this space. The room here becomes a shrine not only celebrating the essences of lives we shall never know, but also the words of the American modernist architect, Louis Kahn – "The room is the beginning of architecture". The scene is set here for the onset of some narrative happening, but which, nevertheless, remains tightly held in the realm of imminence.

Not only does Sighicelli counterbalance reality and fantasy in these images but also the prosaic and the exotic, ambiguity persists here as the light weaves its magic. But here she has some tricks up her sleeve, for these images are back-lit in light boxes, not totally, but partially back-lit. Her C-type prints are mounted on perspex and are selectively masked with black spray paint on the reverse in order to control the amount of light which penetrates the image, muting the light in the darker parts of the image, and allowing the illumination to flood through, amplifying the lighter areas, giving them an almost surreal luminosity, which lends them the air of the uncanny, transforming the ordinary into the remarkable. It is this distinctive use and treatment of light which sharply contrasts Sighicelli's work with that of Bäckström and Lambri. Bäckström similarly uses only available light when taking her images, but they are exhibited as front-lit C-type prints mounted on aluminium, their tones tend to be even and matter-of-fact, with nothing to prove, the light here merely facilitating the documentation of the scene. Lambri uses light as a mediator between viewer and architecture, she has a strong empathy with the moods that are created by the interfaces between incidental light and structural surfaces – she celebrates the use of light as part of the architectural composition – true to its nature, light brings levity into her images. The light here shares the magic of Sighicelli's images; it is not, however, enigmatic or mysterious, but energising.

None of these artists seem to be intimidated by the suggestion that domestic interiors are, stereotypically, the female domain, so that in fact their projects may, in many ways, be deemed as predictable. The feminine, intuitive, perpetuation of the interior as intimate heart and hearth of our lives. Nothing could be further from the truth, however, as the demeanour of these images only serves, as a metaphor, to expose the progressive loss of the home as sanctuary or retreat, infiltrated and permeated as our contemporary Western homes are by the exterior world through the all-pervasive e-media which have now become part of their fabric. This pollution violates the seclusion which is essential for the re-charging of our batteries, and is just as insidious as that "pollution of distances and lengths of time that is degrading our habitat", ascribed to the e-media by Paul Virilio in his book *Open Sky*. The abandoned interiors depicted in the images of Lambri, Bäckström and Sighicelli, exude a sense of loss which serves as a warning, perhaps, that the sanctuary of the archetypal home is fast becoming a part of history.

Elisa Sighicelli, L.A.:Blinds III, 1999

Anne Zahalka
Theory Takes a Holiday

PAVEL BÜCHLER

"Australia is the driest land on earth and spans three time zones... More than a third of the country is classified as desert... The service sector accounts for almost three quarters of GNP... There is a strong agricultural base which contributes 40% of export earnings..." The introduction to *Journeys in the Dreamland*, a recent exhibition which featured the work of Anne Zahalka at Ffotogallery in Cardiff, begins with a few paragraphs which must have been extracted from a geography textbook. How relevant is it to know such realia of the work's place of origin? And why do geopolitical considerations of its antipodean provenance so often greet contemporary art from Australia in Europe and guide its critical reception? Or more to the point, is 'Australia' where Zahalka's work originates? Is it where it belongs? Why should I not, for instance, try to find a central European gene in her photographs, hidden perhaps in what seems like a loose allusion to her Czech father's name in *Leisureland*?[1]

In 1985, Anne Zahalka exhibited a set of photographic tableaux with a title borrowed from an article in a critical journal, *The Tourist as Theorist*. They present a cast of characters from travel brochures and holiday snapshots, in T-shirts and sunglasses, suitcase in hand, camera at the ready, in front of sights from 'elsewhere'. There is the Louvre, Eiffel Tower and London Underground, Florence, Venice, New York and Hollywood, and yes, there is also the Old Town Square in Prague. The *mise-en-scène* is obviously a back-projected image. These are souvenirs from the artist's travels in the hyper-reality of the photographic studio: 'Theory takes a Holiday', the subtitle announces in parentheses, in the photographic practice. The trip to the studio is a journey into a foreign land where the artist, disguised as a native, is herself a stranger. She travels alone, or in the intimate company of her models, sometimes plotting her outings from the map charted by art history, sometimes following the itinerary of pure curiosity. The 'artistic licence' is her passport; 'theory' is perhaps her Baedeker; her pictures are postcards sent back home to show what is 'there' to see.

In *Leisureland*, her most recent project, Zahalka ventures into the territory of visual display, an environment in which images are actively produced, and indeed whole worlds and cultures are invented, rather than viewed with detachment. A miniature railway passes a white-washed mission church before crossing a bridge over a deep mountain gorge. A few crudely painted clouds hover at a discrete distance above a woodland landscape in the background, and the blue of the sky spills over onto the breeze block wall behind. There are some spare landscape parts and landmarks in a polystyrene box tucked away in a cave-like opening in the bowels of the papier-mâché geology. In the *Star City Casino*, the scenario is reversed. A mountain formation is jammed underneath the ceiling of a cavernous subterranean gambling hall. The picture is taken from high above, from where security cameras survey the whirlpools of the roulette tables. It is like the view from *Scenic Skyway* cable car suspended, it seems, from the horizon which separates the real Blue Mountains forest from the real Blue Mountains sky. Except that in this photograph the sky could be a watercolour sketch, the forest in the valley has the texture of the green sponge used by model makers, and the old-fashioned yellow carriage, level with the camera, looks as though it has just been taken out of a toy box and put in this place to turn land into a scenery for the benefit of the photograph.

'Display' is an etymological cousin of 'diaspora'. The scattering, dispersion, cultural displacement of things are the diasporic conditions of display – things unsettled by conflicts of perception and interpretation, uprooted from their familiar relationships by never-ending symbolic violence and chaos. In the culture of visual display, any image is always only provisional. As soon as it is formed, it is absorbed into the flux of complex transactions between appearances and symbols governed as much by the rules of economic and social exchange as by the principles of an indiscriminate cultural import of the old, traditional, rural or ethnic into the new, modern, urban and cosmopolitan, of history into heritage, and even of the futuristic (as another traditional category) into the technological. Or better still, this unstable image is formed on the move, as it were, always between places.

Zahalka's photographs are often staged and always

Scenic Skyway, 1999

Model Railway, 1998

Star City Casino, 1998

constructed with a great deliberation, rather than 'taken' in an unpremeditated instant. She uses photography in its optical capacity, as an instrument of perspective. Her pictures offer a point of view, rather than a 'slice of time'. Like tourist attractions, they deal in the illusions of immediacy and authenticity compromised by photography's own aspirations; like the environments of organised leisure and like leisure pursuits, they are engaged in a reconfiguration of identities and relationships on the threshold of fantasy; and like theories, they are speculative rather than evidential. They show, indeed, what there is to see – as long as the 'there' is not a place but a proposition by the artist intended to make us look. And there we see it, arrested in its transience, in its interminable flow. But what is it?

Zahalka's pictures do not direct us towards 'Australia' or the 'Australian' (except in that banal metaphorical sense in which a stroll down the underwater glass walkway of a marine aquarium in Oceanworld is a trip 'down under'), not least because the logic of display permits no exemptions. Rather, they prompt us to disbelieve any itinerary of departures and destinations.

The slim catalogue which accompanied Zahalka's exhibition *Fortresses and Frontiers* in 1993 may hide a clue. It is made as a conventional spiral-bound picture postcard set. The standard postcard design on the back of each card indicates that these are intended for use. But in the bottom left corner where the addressee's eye turns to verify the sender's location, it will encounter the word 'untitled' under the name of the photographer. This withdrawal of information frustrates the attempt to identify topographic facts and places. For while 'untitled' refers us to the visible, it always contains a warning that things may not be what they seem. Either the pictures are open scenarios which gain their currency as they unfold, or they defy those terms by which connections between appearances and places are established and confirmed. 'Untitled' is not a toponymic category. No place is untitled, but if there is an untitled place without a name, without a nominal identity, then it must be a mirror image of the no-place with a name, or the name without a place, Utopia.

'Untitled No. 11' from the series shows a desolate excavation site, a vacant lot in the centre of a city, with a rim of temporary structures and prefabricated cabins. This large hole in the ground, partly flooded with water, looks like a reflection of the rusty-brown façade crowned with green copper cupolas of the building on its far side. Once grandiose piece of eurocentric colonial architecture, it is now besieged by modern tower blocks. A steel-blue skyscraper at the top and an abandoned red haulage container at the bottom of the frame provide a central axis which, at once, joins the foreground with the background and splits the image in half. This visual symmetry, hierarchy and multiple framing within the frame correspond to the symbolic asymmetries between high-rise luxury and temporary hostel living, the token of bulk transportation of produce and merchandise and the citadel of corporate business, demolition and construction, monumentality and the banality of debris, inducing simultaneously the sense of claustrophobia and vertigo. A small detail ads to the confusion. Almost trimmed off the edge of the picture, there is a steep metal staircase. A sign on the top of the stairs reads: 'No vacancies'.

But all these careful arrangements orchestrated by the artist for our critical pleasure are thrown into disarray by what there is to see. In the original light-box version of the work, the image is saturated with improbable light. The sky is cold blue, the windows of the tower block glow orange, the water is impossibly bright green. It seems to emit light like a pool of poisoned potion from a mystic tale, or like some luminous matter from the fantasies of UFOs and aliens' landings – a treacherous, spell-bound image, not from this world but definitely in it.

We are left transfixed in front of the picture, where we belong and where geography no longer matters.

[1] In Czech, 'zahálka' means 'idleness'.

Five works from Anne Zahalka's 'Fortresses and Frontiers' were shown as part of *Journeys in the Dreamland*, Ffotogallery, Cardiff, February – March 2000, and in a solo exhibition at Robert Sandelson, London, March 2000.

▶

Untitled No. 7a, 1993 *(above)* Untitled No.11, 1993 *(opposite)*

Sharon Kivland
The Scent of a Woman: Between Flesh and Breath

JANE RENDELL

"In general, women are much more interested in others. This can be seen, for example, in the use of transitive verbs with the person as the animate object – 'je le lave' [I wash him], m'aimes-tu?' [do you love me?] – or of prepositions expressing inter-subjectivity; *avec* [with], *entre* [between, amongst], *à* [to], *pour* [for], etc.

"[. . .] Women are more attentive to the question of place: they are close to things, to others (*autres*, which is related to one of the indo-european roots of the verb *etre* [to be])."

(Luce Irigaray, Thinking the Difference: The Athlone Press, London, 1994, pp. 48-49)

Sharon Kivland's *le bonheur des femmes* consists of 24 photographs hung low on the gallery wall. Above them float the names of various famous perfumes: 'Allure', 'Fantasme', 'Knowing', 'Fragile', 'Dazzling', 'Sublime'. The images all show women's feet and legs clad in black from the knees down. This is apparent. But another similarity is not. All the photographs were taken in the same kind of place – at the perfume counters of various shopping venues in Paris: La Samaritaine, Galeries Lafayette, Au Printemps, Bazaar de L'Hotel de Ville. Further, all these female legs are at rest. Pausing. These feet are in touch with the ground. Just.

The making of these images continues the development of themes Kivland has been exploring in her work for a number of years – exchange, consumption and display and the gendering of these relationships. My own research into spaces of consumption in early nineteenth century London brought me into contact with similar spaces and figures: with arcades, shops and shoppers; with Karl Marx, Sigmund Freud, Jacques Lacan and Luce Irigaray, as well as with a rich and complex set of thematics concerning the commercial activity of shopping, the conflation of the female shopper with the commodities she is purchasing, the exchange and use value of femininity, and choreographies of looking and moving in public urban spaces.

Luce Irigaray's seminal essay *Women on the Market* is a key reference point here. Irigaray reworks the marxist analysis of commodities as the elementary form of capitalist wealth to show the ways in which women are commodities in patriarchal exchange – the objects of physical and metaphorical exchange among men. The female commodity has two irreconcilable categories – use value and exchange value. But as well as providing a feminist critique of women's existing position in patriarchy, Irigaray's writing also offers women an utopian position. Her account of exchange suggests to me a dynamic gendering of space, a choreography of mobility and visuality. For Irigaray, female subjectivity is a spatial condition, where the spatiality of the female body metaphorically describes new forms of cultural exchange between men and women as equal but different subjects. The 'between' is important here as a way of imagining these new occupations of space between men and women. The 'between' is offered to us for contemplation in Kivland's images – in both economies of vision and movement.

Acts of looking – voyeurism, narcissism, gazing and fetishisation – and being looked at – exhibitionism, spectacle, masquerade and display – are circuits of complex visual exchanges. Traditional models of psychoanalysis which describe the construction of the gaze in relation to various stages of childhood development, provide a simplistic model: the active male gazer and the passive female spectacle. In visual art practice, the objectifying function of the male gaze can be reinforced by positioning women as the focus of the look within the space of the image. Even at a time when we are keen to reject notions of intentionality, the ways in which we interpret what we see, depends often on what is known of the gender politics of the artist. In Kivland's images we see a repetition of the-body-in-parts – a series of disembodied legs. Does she want us to believe that she is colluding, fetishising the female body by displaying it in bits? Or that she is resisting, refusing the fetishising gaze? These legs are not that sexy after all. Do I ask the same questions of Clifton Steinberg's photographs? An artist who also makes images of women caught in the act, caught

déclaration obsession first allure blonde fantasme amazone dazzling trésor eternity

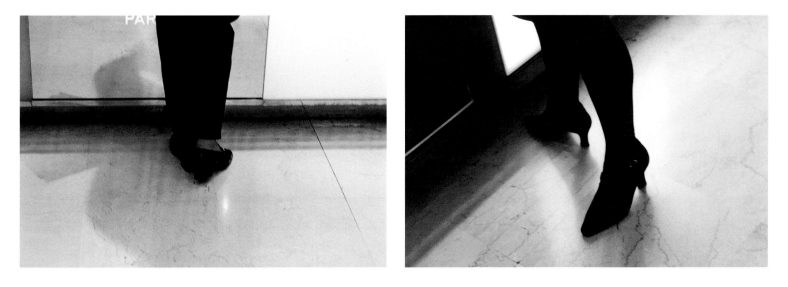

feminine egoiste poison knowing fragile beautiful innocence contradiction infinitif

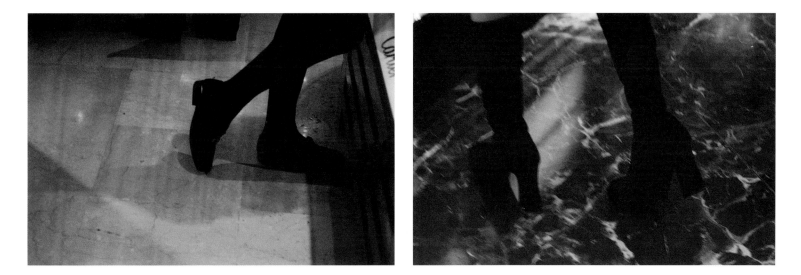

looking at themselves in compact mirrors in arcades?

This raises a series of thoughts about the relationship between women. Between at least three women: a critic, a photographer and her subject matter. Between the gaze of one woman contemplating the gaze of another woman and a-woman-gazed-at. My gazing suggests alternative positions. That there might be different kinds of look; 'gazing' implies authority and surveillance, while 'seeing' allows multiple and different viewpoints. That the distinction made between 'looking' and 'being-looked-at' is a false one; it is almost always possible for reciprocity to occur – even the image looks back. That a woman may 'look' differently from a man – or from any other women for that matter. That a woman may not objectify nor fetishise, and even if she were to, she might well do that differently. And finally, that what is not in the image is as important as what it contains.

Between what is in the image and what is not, a gap is created. A gap between the surface and what lies beyond. For some, woman is surface, femininity is masquerade. But Irigaray's theory of mimicry suggests a conscious strategy for destabilising masquerade. Mimicry is a subversive act which seeks to expose the limitations of the binary oppositions of phallocentric discourse through imitation. A gap appears between the female subject and the feminine sexed identity she is imitating. Are Kivland's photographs like those of Cindy Sherman about this gap? The images have matt surfaces. There is no reflection. No return of the gaze. The woman looks available, but is somehow closed off. The viewer is not allowed to participate fully. Yes, there is a gap, created by the photographer between viewer and subject-to-be-viewed. This gap suggests the act of looking is itself the subject of these photographs.

So far, Kivland's images of women's feet have provided a chance to contemplate the gendering of looking. But they also offer something else. These feet are caught up in another rhetoric. One which is more to do with where they are 'at'.

At the moment these feet are at rest. They have arrived. But, it is inevitable that soon they will leave. Here, they are in-between one place and another. This is not the first time moving women have been present in Kivland's work. They are caught in motion in *Les Passages Couverts* (1998) and in *Mes Peripateticiennes* (1999).

Elsewhere I have argued that mobility is a gendered issue. In the early nineteenth century, women who moved freely on the streets, streetwalkers, were associated with loose morality. Women's movement on the street was controlled through legislation, such the Vagrancy Acts, and through gendered representations of the city, where in the narrative of the fallen women for example, the cause of her eventual destruction was her walking in the city. If we can return to Irigaray briefly. In *On the Market*, Irigaray highlights some patriarchal rules concerning sexual difference and space. Men are active, they move and exchange. Women are passive, they are to-be-exchanged/to-be-moved as commodities between men. Hence, those women who determine their own movement, who perform acts of exchange, who buy and sell, are rule-breakers, are threatening. On other occasions, Irigaray has argued that women's connection with nomadism caused their confinement within the 'prison-house' of the male symbolic order. She suggests a different way of conceptualising women's relation to movement, through the figure of the angel, an alternative to the phallus. The angel is not one but many. She circulates. She mediates between things. The angel is a threshold figure. She goes between.

I would like to end here by considering Kivland's images in terms of the angelic – of what it is to be between. To be at the perfume counter is to be between. To be in a liminal state, a magical space of enchantment where the air is dense with imaginings of who you might become. The anticipated application of a certain scent, the possibilities inherent in its purchase, is a dance between being somewhere and imagining many elsewheres. At the perfume counter, this dance is played out again and again at the very point the scents are allowed to breath, to escape into the air. The juxtaposition of the names of perfumes – all words which suggest desire – hovering just above the images of the grounded feet produces a place between, a gap between two signifiers, between earth and air, flesh and breath, between who we are and who might become.

"The angel is that which unceasingly *passes through the envelope(s) or container(s)*, goes from one side to the other, reworking every deadline, changing every decision, thwarting all representation."

(Luce Irigaray, 'An Ethics of Sexual Difference', London: The Athlone Press, 1993, p. 15).

David Williams
Stillness and Occurrence

Sam Taylor-Wood
Soliloquy

SUSANNA BEAUMONT

"The act of talking when alone or regardless of any hearers". So runs the definition of soliloquy, the word that Sam Taylor-Wood took to title her 1998 series of five photographs, *Soliloquy I-V*. It is a word that suggests a solitary drama: uttering words into empty spaces or entering into reverie unencumbered by the thought of being spectated upon.

The role of spectator is frequently adopted by Taylor-Wood. She may direct and choreograph the 'characters' she photographs or videos, yet there is a sense that she is spectating unseen on to a private world of numerous individuals. For the viewer it creates a palpable feeling of uneasiness. In her 1995 video projection *Brontosaurus*, a man danced unselfconsciously alone and naked. Private abandon is made public. In *Travesty of a Mockery*, a video projection, also from 1995, a couple row in the kitchen. Intimate turmoil is made spectator sport.

Arguably in an age of fly-on-the-wall documentaries, we are well-versed in spectating, without fear of guilt or implication, on the real-life drama of other people's lives. Yet with Taylor-Wood's work we are initially seduced by what we believe to be the inherent 'artificiality' of her characters: we are cajoled into a sense of detachment, imagine an emotional immunity.

In *Soliloquy*, Taylor-Wood plays the role of both spectator and excavator. Each of the five works adopts one compositional template. Below an image of a solitary individual lies in a diorama. Compositionally it echoes Renaissance altarpieces in which a depiction of Christ, the Virgin Mary or a saint was augmented by a predella charting events from the subject's life. Moreover, just as subtitles inform a 'reading' of a film, in *Soliloquy* each diorama informs the viewing of the solitary individual. And it is here that Taylor-Wood acts as excavator: she is exposing what lies beneath the surface, what we imagine to be the subconscious of the individual.

In *Soliloquy I*, a man lies draped on a sofa. His right hand hangs limp. His eyes are closed. We believe him to be asleep, comfortably stationed at that halfway house between life and death. We watch a vulnerability and perhaps wonder what dreams are coursing through his ▶

Soliloquy III, 1998 *(previous page)*, Soliloquy VI, 1999 *(above)*, Soliloquy I, 1998 *(right)*

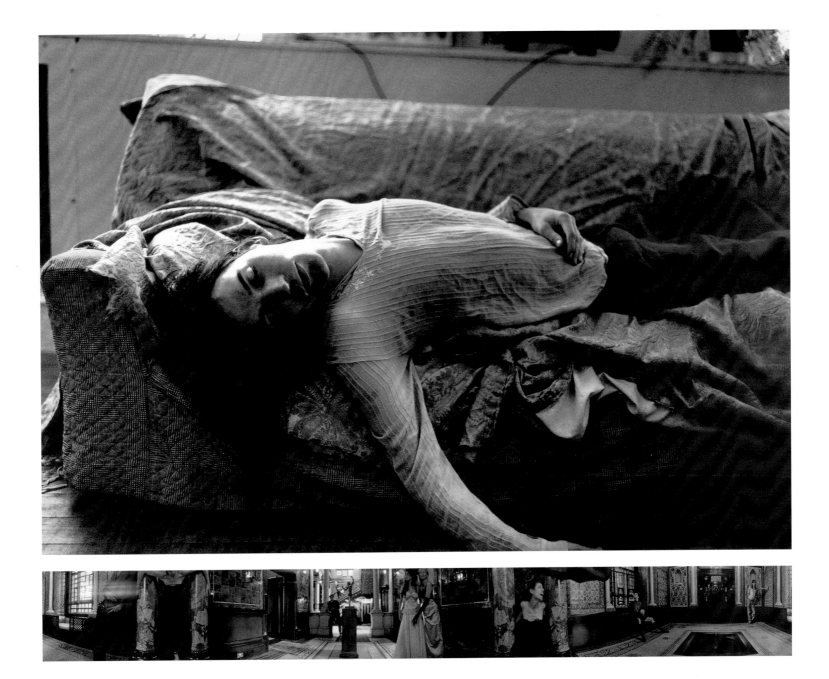

mind. But there is an edge. The man's pose is drawn directly from Henry Wallis' 1854 painting, *The Death Of Chatterton*. Taylor-Wood throws up mirage. Are we looking at a sleeping life or an image of unwakeable death?

Below this recumbent figure lies a diorama of an opulent interior inhabited by opulently dressed men and women. There is a dream-like surreality to the scene. The figures are dwarfed by the larger scale of the figure above, promoting a sense that our view has been squeezed through a keyhole on to an Wonderlandesque landscape of either the subconscious or past reality in a dead man's life.

Taylor-Wood's work beguiles. Frequently she employs a well-ordered, compositional charm similar to that found in 18th century conversation pieces. She replaces decoratively dressed individuals drawn from the ruling classes, who take tea in stately drawings rooms, with thoroughly contemporary characters who inhabit an equally well-appointed and aesthetically nourished modern world. In *Five Revolutionary Seconds*, a series of photographs dating from 1996, a range of interiors are inhabited by stylish clad individuals, but Taylor-Wood's characters are empty of conversation. Saturated with ennui, they are set in isolation and socially frigid. One imagines that they anaesthetise their anxieties with fantasies.

In *Soliloquy II*, we are privy to a fantasy. A man stands bare-chested on an expanse of gravel. The belt of his trousers is undone and he is surrounded by dogs. Dogs that sniff, scratch and lick. There is an ache of wantonness to the scene. Below in the diorama, sexuality is at play in a confined space. Men and women - some naked, some scantily dressed - occupy a glazed tiled room. Similarly in *Soliloquy III*. Here a woman, in the manner of Velazquez's *Venus*, lies naked on a bed and gazes at her reflection in a mirror. A solitary moment of vanity, where gratification is sought through narcissism. Below naked figures are sitting, sauntering, licking and kissing in an airy apartment. But the scene is chilled. This is a perfunctory market place in which to either exhaust or witness desire.

Taylor-Wood creates a world blighted by a communications breakdown. Her characters talk into empty spaces. Where there is dialogue, it is discord. Yet if Taylor-Wood's world is a stage, and all her men and women merely players, there is an unnerving knowingness that any one of us could be about to enter stage right.

Soliloquy II, 1998 *(opposite)*

Paul Seawright
Malevolent Landscapes

MARK DURDEN

Paul Seawright's recent colour photographs of empty and forlorn places, taken on the edges of various European cities, accord with Walter Benjamin's well-known description of Eugène Atget's photographs as deserted, like scenes of a crime. The project began when Seawright was living in Paris and came out of looking at a lot of Atget's pictures. Before moving on to other locations, Seawright started photographing the *terrain vague* of places around Paris's periphérique.

He describes the places in this latest series of photos as "generic malevolent landscapes". They represent the places you would go to if you wanted to dispose of a body. While researching for this work, Seawright discovered that there was some truth in the myth of the shallow grave in the forest: "Bodies are often found covered over in a forest, close to cities, and rarely far from a road." Two pictures from the series give us eerie night shots of woodland on the edge of town. Illuminated by street lighting the trees have an orange colour: the effect is filmic, lurid lighting dramatises the scene, shifts the pictures away from the more evidentiary and literal look of others in the series. Many pictures invite close inspection, as we look for clues, evidence of something untoward. Ordinary things become charged with potential meaning as a result – the trampled down vegetation edging a white brick embankment, for example, or a shaft made dangerous with its inspection cover removed.

Such recent pictures return us to his first major work, *Sectarian Murder*, 1988. A number of sectarian killings occurred during an upsurge of violence in the early seventies, and over a decade and half later the artist visited the sites where the bodies of the victims had been discovered, locations which sometimes coincided with the sites of the killings. Born in Belfast, Seawright was brought up at the height of the 'Troubles' in the seventies, and in some sense this work is about the atmosphere of fear and mistrust which marked his childhood. Colour views of parks, tourist spots, building sites, wastegrounds, are combined with matter of fact texts taken from news reports detailing sectarian murders. The captioning texts serve to give narrative to the 'landscapes', change our relation to them. Seawright has removed historical details from the texts, victims are not defined as Loyalist or Republican, Protestant or Catholic. The sense of a randomness to the killing is further brought out as a result. With some, the colour and view contradicts the sinister events which took place there, and with others the places seem appropriate sites for dumping bodies or committing murders – these latter in particular link up with his recent series of malevolent landscapes. And, as in Seawright's latest pictures, not all the photographs in *Sectarian Murder* are literal, one mimes the point of view of an assassin, as we view the spot of a murder through a car window. The matter of fact record of place is embellished, dramatised.

Many of the pictures rest upon the chilling aura of crime scene photographs and play upon the indexical impact and import of photography. While Seawright arrives at the scene of the crime much too late for there to be signs of what once took place there, his photographs are caught up in the way places are haunted by past events. He has spoken of these pictures in relation to evidence photographs taken by the New York City Police Department during the early part of the twentieth century – discovered and published by the writer Luc Sante – particularly the uninhabited crime photos rich with implication: the footprints in snow lit up by flash in the night shot of a parkland where someone was shot.[1] If *Sectarian Murder* abstracted the political dimensions of the killings, and we did not know from what side we viewed the crimes – Loyalist or Republican. With the series of photographs which make up both *The Orange Order*, 1991, and *Police Force*, 1995, we are given compelling close-up details of the view from one side, a privileged insider's view of the dominant power forces in Northern Ireland. For Seawright, such work is "a sort of personal archaeology – coming to terms with my Protestant history and the whole notion of inherited generational politics." The first series shows us the symbolic rituals of the Orange Order which are legible in terms of power and authority, while the second detail the weapons, interiors and dress of the RUC. As I write, the British media, focused on IRA decommissioning, gives little attention to the military might

Untitled (Forest, Night) 1999

From the series Fires, Belfast, 1997

Untitled (Black Spike), 1997 *(above)*   Cage II, 1997 *(overleaf)*

of the RUC in Northern Ireland. Nothing changes. As John Pilger pointed out, during the 1994-96 IRA ceasefire both press and broadcast coverage adhered strictly to the British government model. "'Decommissioning' of IRA arms became a major issue... while minimal attention was paid to the Unionist paramilitaries..."[2] Seawright's *Missing* series – commissioned by the Nederlands Foto Institut and Mondrian Foundation of Holland in 1997 – is perhaps best seen as the antithesis of both *The Orange Order* and *Police Force*. It follows on from work made in 1995 about the disappeared, those abducted by the IRA in the seventies and never seen again. With *The Missing*, the form is the same as both *The Orange Order* and *Police Force*, a similar succession of close-up fragmentary details. Only they do not point to a fixed symbolic order, instead of an obsessive detailing of the insignia of power the pictures offer up realist details of the disempowered, testify to a loss of identity. Many of the pictures in *Missing* function metonymically, we link the missing subjects to abject close-up details of oily meatballs, a half-eaten sandwich, the dirty overgrown nails of someone's hands. Even details showing the homeless washing themselves seem to accord with this sense of dirtiness. The photograph of empty waste ground in the series becomes legible as the (non) place of the homeless. Seawright in many senses is trading on familiar 'documentary' signs of the other in this series. Only he gives us blow ups of these signs in the form of a succession of abject details. Reading such pictures in opposition to both *The Orange Order* and *Police Force*, I am reminded of the tension set up between Andres Serrano's two series of portraits, of Nomads and Klan members, both of 1990 and often exhibited together. Only with Serrano's pictures, tatty threads often undermine the ritualised self-presentation of the hooded members of the Ku Klux Klan and the homeless are romanticised and idealised through dress and pose. Seawright's *The Orange Order* contains no aberrant details, no loose seams, just an immaculate order.

The Missing leads to Seawright's latest series of landscapes in European cities, which also attempts to move away from the specificity of his Northern Ireland work. His most recent photographs nevertheless bear continuities and links with his series of photographs taken on the 'Peace Line' in Belfast, in 1997. His recent solo show at Interim Art mixed pictures from both series. In this exhibition, fire or the evidence of fire in the two Belfast photos offered up an image of a dramatised landscape – clearly symbolic of Seawright's conflict-ridden homeland – while the European pictures appeared more understated,

deadpan they awaited and expected the viewer to give them drama. The more powerful pictures from the Belfast series are those which simply present us with frontal views of the entrances to pubs which have been turned into fortresses, caged for protection since they are vulnerable to attack because of their location on the edge of Protestant and Catholic communities.

In turning his camera upon vacant places on the edges of various European cities, Seawright's recent photographs bear formal affinities with Willie Doherty's recent work in Northern Ireland. Both artists mime a forensic mode of looking and trade on the connotative potential of waste and derelict ground as the place where it is assumed violent acts are likely to have taken place. Doherty also uses handheld video, extending his forensic gaze to a protracted searching of wastegrounds. Such videos play upon our fantasies and desires for a gruesome discovery. But instead all we get are occasional glimpses of domestic waste and rubble.

Seawright's recent emptied-out European photographs also show us little, but play upon our expectations. The work seems to rest not so much on what is shown, but the fantasies which are triggered by what is shown. This latest series entails a shift geographically away from his homeland, reflecting as he has said a concern that Northern Ireland does not have a monopoly on violence. Not anchored to a specific place, the pictures seek a general anxiety of place, but do so through continuing a forensic mode of looking which emerges as a distinctive aesthetic in connection with the landscape of Northern Ireland.

1. Seawright was also interested in the old superstition with which scene of the crime photography was apparently once caught up: the belief that if the eyes of a murder victim were photographed then you could see the face of his or her assassin within the pupil. The London photographer, William H. Warner, in the 1860s claimed to have taken a photo of the eye of a calf and to have found within it the boards of the slaughterhouse floor.

2. So, if we are to see a political dimension to these pictures it comes about through the way they draw attention to the power of the RUC. Yet at the same time the pictures are caught up – through their fetishising aesthetic – in a troubling seduction with this very power.

Patricia Macdonald
Emergent Landscapes

JAMES LAWSON

We sometimes think that art proves itself by its ability to manipulate its audience. The arts of the theatre and lectern, emblematically speaking, control the thought and feeling of the audience. But art does not need to be so purposeful in its address.

As well as being a matter of addressing an audience, Patricia Macdonald's art is an ongoing account of her thinking about the world. As such, it presents itself as a text for the observer to explore. It is also, in a sense, an exploration for the artist, for she too makes discoveries. She observes that, "After completing a new piece – and this cannot happen too soon after making it – I find it interesting to try to articulate what I think it means – rather like analysing a dream – as a jumping-off point for what comes next." To this extent, her work can be regarded as 'in progress'.

Thinking, learning and communicating, together comprise the art. Patricia Macdonald, by inclination and background – her education is in the natural sciences and the fine arts – is able to cross the boundaries of the 'two cultures'. At the same time, reason and imagination cease to be irreconcilable mental faculties within her practice, and neither is exclusive to one domain. In particular, the making of theories about the world – the activity of the scientist – and the making of possible worlds – that of the artist – become interchangeable when we see that both, preconditionally, set the word 'if' at the beginning of perception. There, what we ordinarily distinguish as fact and fiction pass into a common realm of possibility. This is territory that Patricia Macdonald explores:

"I'm interested in uncertainty, paradox and complexity and in the ongoing search for a 'pattern which connects'.[1] I sometimes work with fragments of poetry and 'magical realist' texts from writers like Rilke, Yeats, Cavafy, Milosz, Levi and Calvino. I'm also influenced by the ideas forming the emerging 'organicist' paradigm or world view[2] which is replacing the 'mechanist' one of modernism and which better describes complex and living systems."

Ostensibly, the individual aerial photograph, dependent as a configuration upon the three spatial coordinates of the camera, conforms with data given to sense rather than processed by intellect. However, the circumstances of Patricia Macdonald's aerial photography call into question that simple understanding.

Flight represents an extreme degree of mobility for vision. When we think about this mobility as we look at the image, the fact of the point of view takes on an arbitrariness. Vision, thought of not as stationary, as in the one-point perspective system, but as mobile, sees things with the properties of the diagram. The diagram – one of the scientist's visual tools – could be described as the point-of-view-less representation. A map can be thought of similarly, as a representation of a landscape within which all distances are 'true' (distances being what the one-point perspective system distorts, because all lines of sight from the observer to the plane of representation are not equal).

If the diagram reveals processes that are 'encoded' in the conventional one-point perspective image, the one is intimated in the other. It is the observer's part to perform the switch. Patricia Macdonald appreciates the flux, the nature of the world as process, and is interested in the means that have been developed for the representation of the most complex processes – those of living systems. Acknowledgement of their diagrammatic representation becomes part of the evolving programme of the artist. As the aeronautical observer, with that especially privileged sense of vision as mobile within the three dimensions of space, she can think of herself as shiftingly located with regard to the origin of the coordinates of such a diagrammatic version of the world. The world to which she addresses herself, is of endlessly changing aspect.

It is partly in order to make the special character of mobility of vision and its implications explicit that Patricia Macdonald has recently been making composite pieces. These have not always been presented as-it-were as a simultaneous multiplication of viewpoints upon the one motif. In works such as *The Sonnets to Orpheus* (1995) and the two series: *Change of State* (1990-) and *The Levels* (1990-) – which can be thought of as non-linear narratives of transformation – the images are to varying degrees diverse. The seven-part work, *The Mirages* (1992-93) ▶

Double-page spreads from book: *Once in Europa*, John Berger and Patricia Macdonald
with Angus Macdonald, pilot *(above and overleaf)*

forms a *single* landscape.[3] Her experimentation with the composite mode of representation continues in the most ambitious and evolved piece of this kind, *The play grounds, no. 6: burnt moorland: grouse shooting, Perthshire, Scotland* (1998). She looks back upon this recent work:

> "This is a grouse-moor – a deadly board-game – seen simultaneously in various spatial ways and from –– various points of view, including that of the grouse. It deals with ideas of freedom and constraint, of hunting and being hunted, and with different systems of perception. It contrasts two superimposed versions (actual and conceptual) of the linear, mechanist grid of modernism with, on the other hand, the non-linear, circling feedback loops of the 'strange attractor', one of the mathematical 'signatures' of the emerging organicist paradigm."

Within the grids and between them are sequences, now elided, now fractured. The whole work is of an exploding perspective at the same time as the fragments belong to the one piece of land. As the world turns and rears and slides away beneath the eye of the camera, pattern shifts and persists.

The same paradoxical state of things pertains in reality. To see ostensibly incompatible things at once is the necessary condition for being able to grasp, in some measure, complex systems in the natural world, including living systems; they change and they remain the same. It is also to see text. The nature of text is that it lies upon and is inseparable from what is present in the literal sense, as interpretative possibility. To acknowledge a sensational object at the same time as to deny it, by treating it as a channel to metaphor or allusion, something essentially elsewhere, is to embrace paradox and grasp text. Surface and depth in images makes of them texts of this kind.

Clearly, there can be no text without a reader or observer. Uncertainty too does not dispense with its observer. Patricia Macdonald, in a recent collaboration with John Berger, has been able to demonstrate, with especial incisiveness, the transformational power that the reader and observer possesses. They have produced a new edition of Berger's story, *Once in Europa*[4], the central, pivotal element of his trilogy, *Into their Labours*. Patricia Macdonald outlines the story:

> "An old woman from a mountain peasant community is given an 'aerial baptism' by her pilot son. As they fly together over the harsh yet voluptuous landscapes in which she has spent her life, and which have been

changed in every sense by the arrival of a huge electro-metallurgical factory complex, we hear her thoughts and see through her eyes and her mind's eye – a mixture of sensation and memory, of the overview and the intimate, which all come together as she makes sense of her life."

The collaboration produces a work in which written narrative and photographic images are integrated into a new fabric. In it, we discover the huge power of narrative and image, when brought into these precise conjunctions, to skew one another, bringing each into pointed focus and opening the channels of metaphor that lie beneath their surfaces. The forces that shape the lives of the people in the story and the world in which they live are laid before us here.

Seeing is a complicated activity, one that oscillates between observation – attempting to see things as they are – and what we may call imagination – recognising that things are as thinking and feeling makes them. That is the beginning of Patricia Macdonald's work; thinking about the world and herself as its transformative witness.

1 Bateson, G, *Mind and Nature*, Dutton, New York, 1979

2 See for example, Prigogine, I & I Stengers, *Order out of chaos*, Flamingo, London, 1985; Maturana, H & F Varela, *The tree of knowledge*, Shambala, Boston, 1987. For useful syntheses, Thompson, W I, *Gaia. 2 : Emergence: the new science of becoming*, Lindisfarne, New York, 1991; Capra, F, *The web of life: a new synthesis of mind and matter*, Flamingo, London, 1997

3 See Macdonald, P, 'To remain dissolved: aspects of photography and language', *Studies in Photography: The Scottish Society for the History of Photography*, 1996, pp. 24-35 and Dorrian, M, 'The middle distance: on the photography of Patricia Macdonald', *Katalog*, Vol.11, no. 2, pp. 2-11, Odense, 1999

4 Berger, J & P Macdonald, with Angus Macdonald, pilot, *Once in Europa*, Bloomsbury, London, 1999

All Patricia Macdonald's aerial images are made in collaboration with Angus Macdonald as pilot.

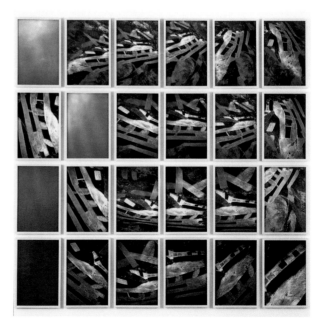

The play grounds series, no.6: burnt moorland, grouse shooting (24-part work)
Perthshire, Scotland, 1998 and detail *(opposite)*

Garry Fabian Miller
Petworth Windows

DAVID ALAN MELLOR

Some mighty power of halation – with light bending around cruciform window frames and blinds – is at work in and drives Garry Fabian Miller's new series of photographs. A spiritual history seems imminent in them, where light dictates a moral moment, like the invocation to sublime illumination in Barnett Newman's paintings. There is a definite history to this kind of allegorical luminist sublimity; it also functions in J.M.W. Turner's painting *Regulus*, a large oil picture of a blinded noble Roman juxtaposed with a glaring ribbon of dazzling light. He painted this in the year of Lord Egremont's death: Egremont had been Turner's patron and had let him live for extended periods at his country home, Petworth House, where he had worked on apotheoses of light and landscape. It was an acknowledgement of this interest in this abiding topic of light as an idealised prime and foundational signifier which led to the artist Garry Fabian Miller being appointed as Artist in Residence at Petworth House last year, as part of a project organised by the agency PhotoWorks in conjunction with The National Trust.

Inserted into history in this fashion, Miller ran the risk of functioning in an anachronistic fix, of being an illustrator trudging in the footsteps of a shining moment in English cultural history in the nineteenth century. But his new series, *Petworth Windows*, while citing the site of Turner's painting from the terrace and windows of Egremont's country seat, also transposes that nineteenth century luminism into the frame of certain twentieth century Modernist protocols of manipulating light and forms of universal abstract spiritualism. The cultural and geo-contextualism of Petworth is tempered by the halated shadows of Man Ray and Moholy Nagy, but it is also contingent on Miller's own schemes of spiritual representation.

The elementary geometries of *Petworth Windows* look towards an aspiration to spectral light which speaks of the condition of its own making, in the darkroom. Miller passes a beam of light across the darkroom, through a lens which is a blue glass container with water in it, filled to the top and forming a curved meniscus as the refracting medium – he

had been intrigued by the domestic pots in Fox Talbot's home. This aqueous light is then processed through a screen of cardboard obstructions and on to the cibachrome paper on the wall. If this glances at the lunar passes of Man Ray, it also conjures up those narratives of Isaac Newton in a darkened room, half alchemist, half experimental scientist, decomposing light into the spectrum. The light which produces these testimonies of being touched and tinged by these arcane processes which Miller has contrived is more than self-reflexively demonstrating its own condition: the performance, he says, produces a peculiar blue-white light which has specific associations for him. Miller's spiritualised pastoralism is well-known and he has spoken of a wish to make pictures which correspond to his experience of walking on his native Dartmoor at night and being aware of the residual light that remains in the night sky when it is apparently dark.

This fugitive light is, for Miller, tied in with the way in which recent biographies have recounted a heart-rending episode at the time of Turner's death: more than this, Miller credits it for the entire inception of the *Petworth Windows* series. Turner attempted to crawl – in these narratives – from his deathbed, towards the window of the room he was in and towards the light. This mortal progress of a body towards light has embedded itself in Miller's mind as a poetic model of spiritual performance and one which might be enacted by the spectator's eyes in trying to seek out the unearthly, vestigial light which is screened off from our gaze. The blinds that are hiding the light are not simply obstacles; their forms come heavily coded: on the one hand in terms of a history of a particular descent of Modernism with which Miller identifies – the braced chambers of Mondrian or the crosses of Malevich. On the other hand, the ladders of ascension and the crosses point to a Christian iconography: no forms are more over-determined than the crucifix). The halated light which emanates from these dye destruction prints is concealed and conceals a numinous body. It is, according to the hymn, "...only the splendour of light [which] hideth thee".

Jem Southam
The Shape of Time

DAVID CHANDLER

Living and working from Exeter, Jem Southam's photographic work of the last twenty years has been informed by his fascination with the coastal and rural topography of the South West of England, a place where geological history, social and industrial narratives and myth are densely interwoven. The physical exploration of this cultural landscape, and a sense of discovery are vital to his work, but so too is Southam's intellectual curiosity, one that finds connections over a broad range of disciplines. Although his work is firmly 'located', grounded within a particular regional and even domestic context, with things close to home, Southam's explicit concern has been to find a metaphorical imagery and a language that invokes an unbounded space, that refers to global as well as personal events, and that can provide a vehicle for the scientific, social and aesthetic themes that motivate his practice.

Southam's latest works, brought together under the collective title *The Shape of Time*, have been made since October 1994 at over twenty sites in the South and South West, where he has observed and recorded three particular land formations: cliff rock falls, river mouths and estuaries, and dew ponds. In contrast to the catalogue of chance encounters that made up his last complete work, *The Raft of Carrots* from 1992, the new work has developed along more programmatic, analytical lines into distinctive series, and further into photographic sequences based around the collection of data and the measurement of change.

Despite the kind of statuesque calm that settles over the sites, despite the beautifully subdued colour range and the largely absent social traces that might fasten them securely to the present, Southam's new images are not 'time-less' landscapes and they offer us little reassurance. Each chosen site is in continual flux, and from the dramatic as well as minor disturbances he describes, Southam unveils a land that is unstable and unpredictable, constantly moving through different states and at varying speeds. These entropic processes are the underlying 'subject' of his pictures and, charted from image to image, they draw in and hold his attention while testing the descriptive and narrative potential of the still photograph.

But this watching and describing also cradles a sense of unease. For Southam, the earth's instability and degenerative processes suggest other forms of upheaval and uncertainty, both social and personal, and again both dramatic and more slowly insistent. His photographs might also be read as visions of collapse and slippage that mirror similar residual fears in the human psyche, those that link – often through dreams – sudden or appalling shifts in fate to cataclysmic natural events. And yet, while the work taps into to a reservoir of anxiety, it clearly demonstrates that processes of change also harbour reconfiguration and renewal, and another strand of Southam's work celebrates the ways in which the complex systems of the landscape, and by implication those of social and personal relations too, find new and workable patterns of life.

Southam's dew ponds are points of intensity in the landscape. From picture to picture Southam records their evolving appearance: through changes in water levels, surface patina, wind direction, or in the growth and decay of vegetation. Following these changes intently, and scanning the picture's minute textural details, we sense that every element, each blade of grass, each wildflower, each mound and gully, contributes to a balance that determines seasonal renewal and allows the ponds to dry up and reappear. But, in addition to this density of matter, Southam's images are similarly laden with portent. Like wells, these ponds conceal their depth, they appear like surface wounds opening into the earth's core. Paradoxically, given their relatively recent construction, they seem archaic, evoking the site of some ancient event or ritual; a welcome source of water or maybe a trap, the ponds seem to beckon with an ambiguous promise. In Native American mythology ponds are the eyes of the earth, for Southam they suggest the craters formed by meteor impacts.

The idea of this threat from space, of a potential catastrophe that is both mythic and real, was an important point of departure for Southam's new work. His rock fall photographs expose a threat latent in the landscape and again they combine a sense of menace, an awe-struck response to the violent episode, with the more scientific ▶

Lower Greensands, Whale Chine, Isle of Wight, February 2000

Blind Yeo, Clevedon, Somerset *(dyptich)* January 2000

Ditchling Beacon, from the series Sussex Dew Ponds, November 1999

Newtimber, from the series Sussex Dew Ponds, November 1999

collection of data. The photographs dwell on a formal dialogue embodied in the sculptural form of the land slip, in which the vertical movement down and out of the fallen rocks (precipitated by water moving through the cliff's strata) is in contrast to the horizontal, incoming motion of the tides and winds that cause the erosion. It is a process that represents and brings together vastly different scales of time and movement; where climatic and tidal change intrude on the imperceptible passage of geological time and where a continual seething migration of particles unfolds over and within the more dramatic and massive movement of rock. Southam's image sequences, with their repeated photographic instants, reinforce this collision of natural events and time scales.

As hard evidence of destructive forces at work, Southam's rock fall images come closest to the traditional form of a photographic report, to photography as witness. They have the look of active war zones, but also, like the ponds, they seem the locus of some primal energy. Their resonance is other worldly too, bringing to mind Lunar and Martian landscapes that, in turn, echo back to the brutalised landscapes of war, recalling perhaps Roger Fenton's battlefield photographs of the Crimea or some anonymous wire photograph from the Iraqi desert.

The rate at which the rock fall material is reclaimed by the sea varies from a matter of hours to many years, and while there is something cleansing about this irregular process, there is something haunting, too, in its inevitability. The sweeping motion of the sea is benign, but also invasive and enveloping. In contrast to the wounds and scars inflicted on the land, submergence comes with a sense of finality.

What locates Jem Southam's interest in his series of river mouth and estuary photographs is the idea of confluence, again a merging of energies and types of movement to be detected in the sea and with visible consequences for the land. At each river mouth site new landscapes are made and revealed daily and Southam's image sequences detail every fresh topographical mark, every rivulet or altered contour of sand and pebble, with the precision of a map maker. Uniquely in this series Southam also tracks movement within the photographic time of each exposure. Across the surface of the water his photographs locate the churning of tide and river currents moving over, across and through each other, while at the water's edge the camera's rendition of waves lapping and breaking provides a translucent velvet boundary between land and sea. The photographs also distinguish subtle changes in colour as the sea sweeps up and discharges shore particles and sediment, or as it absorbs and reflects ambient light.

Across the river mouth sites the structures that people have erected to contain, navigate or simply gauge the impact of the sea appear as remnants or relics, giving the shoreline a sense of pathos, while making a fragile graphic counterpoint to the brooding presence of the sea that regularly in Southam's photographs threatens to engulf the viewer.

The constant ebb and flow, the languid and surging motion of the sea that floods and subsides is a restless rhythm given solid form over the land. The river mouth and estuary sites are scoured, rounded and washed over; overwhelmed and constantly unsettled, they aptly characterise Southam's notion of material flux but can also be viewed as analogous to a state of mind, or perhaps to a way of looking that is in some sense extended, like a current flowing slowly through and between many ideas and associations. In this way these characteristics might also be seen to give form, or shape, to particular conceptions of time and history, ones that are fluid and expansive rather than linear, based around slow imperceptible movements and accumulations.

For Southam, both in terms of what the images represent and for his art in general, the still photograph is one pause in a relentless process of change. The photograph refers to what led to it and what leads away from it, whether that is a rock particle, a person or the constantly eroding motion of the tide. It refers to the previous picture and to the next. What the still image might be said to represent in Southam's work is an infinitely complex network of journeys, sliding across and through each other in very different registers of time and space and over a huge range of macro and micro scales.

(This is an edited version of an essay from the book Jem Southam, Rockfalls, Rivermouths + Ponds, published by the Towner Art Gallery and PhotoWorks, April 2000.)

Susanne Ramsenthaler
Timelines

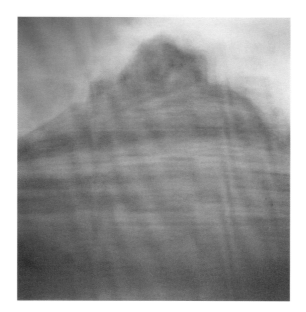

A photograph, we presume, represents a 'moment' in time. Subconsciously, we imagine this moment to be short enough to arrest motion – 1/60th of a second, for example.

The photograph allows us to look in detail at a moment in the past, both as historical enquiry or, if we made the photograph ourselves or were present at the time it was taken, as a trigger for memory.

This regular photograph comes reasonably close to the way we see, or rather, to how we think we see. The conscious eye does not 'see' with selective focus, but darts about continuously, bringing into focus everything it settles on even just for a fraction of a second. The impression is one of overall sharpness in the field of vision. Selective focus in an image, therefore, is a uniquely photographic language which we have learnt to accept and interpret without even thinking.

What happens if the boundaries of this 'photographic moment' are stretched? Before the beginning of the 20th century, light sensitive emulsions were slow and photographers had to use tripods for sharpness during the necessary long exposures. Of course, any moving thing would register as a blur, if it registered at all. City streets were rendered devoid of people, except for the odd stationary person.

Today, the use of a pinhole camera mimics this situation: although film material is much faster now, the aperture (pinhole) is so small as to require a lengthy exposure time, producing similar effects. The photographic 'moment' can last hours, days even. How does this compare to our experience of seeing? Instead of the photograph representing one 'slice' in an ongoing narrative, the narrative has been recorded in, or rather compressed onto, one photograph. This is not something we can experience, or 'see', no matter how hard we try.

Here I am interested in how and what photography can record: images that differ from human experience and perception: what things would look like if we could see that way. Curiously, the traditional roles of photograph and caption are reversed: the images form the 'looser' element, but yet contain everything the more concise captions describe – and much more. *Timelines* compresses space as well as time: covering distances from a quarter of a mile onwards. The human eye's perception exists within these images as layers of palimpsests to be merged and covered by a continuous stream of visual information, eventually forming the finished entity: one photograph. Even the best of eye-games do not come close.

Susanne Ramsenthaler

Keren Amiran
Art as Pause

STELLA SANTACATTERINA

"There is more freedom inside the narrow limit of the particular fragment than the infinite kingdom of Utopia, as the spirit of the modern imagines it."

Hugo von Hofmannsthal

The work of Keren Amiran is rooted and developed within this concept of von Hofmannsthal. The artist shows a lucid attitude towards the world and the elaboration of her work: art can no longer be a privileged production of its own language, nor a creative activity of constructing the image or aesthetic object, but rather an encounter with the world based upon a project of critical reflection, an individual strategy, which intercedes in and prohibits reality. Because art is nothing more than the language of art, the artist is aware of the pathetic hope for art to be understood as a shadow or double of reality, and therefore to escape from its own metaphor and open into the space of the metonymic. The metaphor, the use of the image, is born in fact from the illusion of the presence of the world inside language; instead, metonymic space lives in the awareness of the absence of the world and the impossibility of its being represented through the language of art. So, from a fundamentally synthetic attitude, which tends to organise language according to its own image and resemblance (or simulacrum of the world), we enter into a relation with a critical praxis that gives attention to the organisation and elaboration of its own instruments. Thus, according to Italo Calvino, "...the proper use of language... is one that enables us to approach things (present or absent) with discretion, attention, and caution, with respect for what things (present or absent) communicate without words."

One of the artist's earlier works, *Floor*, 1998, in which she overlaid half the gallery floor with the exact same tiles, presented a mimesis similar to the apparent duplication of an exterior referent of the photographic image. But this minimal gesture of superimposition, through the small gap between the original floor and its simulacrum created a spatio-temporal distance, a dynamic between work and world in which the former is constantly in a state of neutralising itself. The artist founds the work of art in an intermediary space between attentiveness and a discretion to the point of disappearance, in order to produce an active moment of thought. Thus, the work presents itself as a visual tautology, recognisably outside any motivation of eccentricity. Her work tends to introduce an idea of the new as a construction on the already constructed, as a different repetition, which allows an internal pause, or interval, to take place as a shift rather than a sudden, radical transformation *de novo*. This relationship between the new and the transformation is linked with the idea of belonging (to a place, a tradition, a culture and so forth), a progression that is opposed to the idea of a *tabula rasa*. This is most clearly demonstrated in the series of four photographs, *The Family*, 1997, in which each family member is associated with a well known avant-garde artist, thereby linking the domestic family to the 'family of art': 'My Grandfather as Bernd Becher', 'My Grandmother as Hilla Becher', 'My Father as Sigmar Polke', 'My Mother as Hanna Höch'. And yet this declaration of belonging to the family of art is also a way of recognising the flexible territory of art in a particular history, in which time and space function through common logic. This form of appropriation, that is, the attribution of the name of one person to another's face, in this case the artist's real family, again opens a gap; it makes evident to us that the photograph presents a fictionalised persona, or the persona as a mask. Thus, the gap does not conform to the 'primitive' taboo where the name is not an external label but an integral part of the personality; nor does it conform to the Freudian schema where the other is always an ancestor; where the soul is never one's own, but belongs to the 'Father', which is the meaning of the Oedipal complex. On the contrary, once again, this distance concerns the relationship between the subject and language; the persona as mask draws our attention to the fact that a person doesn't possess its own person but always an other by which it is possessed, and this is none other than language itself.

This concept is addressed in a further work, *Ahad Ha'am* (Hebrew meaning 'one of the people'), a series of photocopied colour photographs of all the streets in Israeli cities bearing the name Ahad Ha'am, except the one most familiar to the artist in Tel Aviv. The rationale was that the

1. Kiryat Atta

2. Azur

3. Netanya

4. Kiryat Shmona

5. Sderot

6. Kfar Saba

7. Akko

8. Tiberias

9. Rishon Le-Zion

Ahad Ha'am, *1999*

familiarity of the one formed a pretext for wandering into less familiar territories of the country. The name 'Ahad Ha'am' was the alias of a Zionist Jew writing at the turn of the 19th century, who became important as one of the people who constructed the idea of the Zionist state. In common with most state manoeuvres with regards to national heroes, his popular, assumed name became used to name new suburban streets; and yet, as the artist's work makes explicit, this name, contrary to its assumed role of marking the individual, points, in the banal sameness of these collective photographic views, to its lack of individuality.

Ahad Ha'am claimed he was not a writer as such, but concerned only with the problems of his people, a position with which Keren Amiran has some sympathy: "In some ways I am comparing his attitude as a writer and my own attitude to photography, my use of photography as an artist. I am not a photographer and have no intention... and only by chance, a concerned artist..." The artist's use of the name is close to the strategy of Duchamp's ready-made, which tends to introduce into the object another level of thought, shifting it into a different symbolic order. However, this is opposed to the undifferentiated use of the ready-made as image or object of Pop Art, and even further from the appropriation strategies of the contemporary art scene, where the ready-made produces simply an iconic surplus value comparable to advertising and the telematic image. In Amiran's work, vision is freed of all inessential elements, founding a discipline of the image, which is not repressive but liberated from representation although not from sense. It wields the weapon of suspicion and doubt against the aesthetic, allowing the work to go beyond the anticipated criteria of convention to create a suspension, or syncope, that induces a disequilibrium of meaning. As Barthes says, "the goal of Harmony is neither to further the conflict (by associating through similitude), nor to reduce it (by sublimating, sweetening or normalising the passions), nor yet to transcend... but to exploit it for the greatest pleasure of all and without hindrance to anyone. How? By playing at it: by making a text of the conflictual."

In this sense, the artist's attitude expresses the idea of art as a nomadic intelligence that understands identity as diversity. It consists in the exercise of a critical activity, in which the work becomes a tool for the emergence of a new visibility, for bringing into focus the previously unthought. In this way, the image becomes minimal, reduced to its conceptual necessity. The use of the ready-made image, taken from the architectonic landscape, or the archive of cinema, is born nevertheless of a dynamic of the language that requires the verisimilitude and material presence of an essential vision capable of giving authority to the work. Only in this way can the artist navigate with an ethical security in the territory of art, because the work carries a formal order that justifies the *mise-en-scène* and guarantees the result.

The *mise-en-scène* adopted by the artist in *Psycho*, 2000, is a sequence of small, paired photographic stills taken from the two versions of the film Psycho (Alfred Hitchcock, 1960, and Gus van Sant, 1998). The artist began with a selection of images from the Hitchcock version, which form the right–hand part of the pair, with matching scenes from the later, colour version on the left hand. The extraction of stills from cinematic movement produces a shift away from the narrative towards the iconicity of the image. The comparison between the two similar shots highlights the closeness that Hitchcock's image bears to pictorial traditions. But his images also reflect what Roland Barthes described as the photographic punctum as that moment when the image is able to strike, to arouse questioning, to act as a stimulus to the imagination and go beyond established confines. By contrast, the van Sant still holds no more memorable authority than the casual snapshot of the everyday. Through this comparison, the artist underlines the artifice of the language of representation, as was also understood by Hitchcock, against the assumption of naturalism, which is the condition of contemporary Hollywood cinematic convention. This tendency to insist that the image possess a referent in the 'real world' is also endemic to much contemporary art. Art that attempts to present itself as a reflection of concrete 'reality', of the 'here and now', lacks precisely that suspension or distance of time that allows the exercise of the viewer's own memory and experience, such that reality itself diminishes the work. To 'show all', to show only what is known, is to leave nothing to the imagination. This is contrary to the process of both Amiran and Hitchcock, who begin with representation as a fictional language. Amiran's critical language stresses the responsibility of the creative work, the value of its own historical condition, in which individual imagination is enabled to give form to a language outside any explicit evidence.

The artist's journey follows a circular trajectory, but is never repetitive. The space of art becomes a kind of selection from the flux of the everyday; a movement from quantity to quality; the affirmation of a sense of place – rhythm – which only art can give. What this means is to accept art as clarified vision – a shift from the noise and vulgarity of the media towards an exemplary silence.

portfolio

the catalogue of contemporary photography in britain

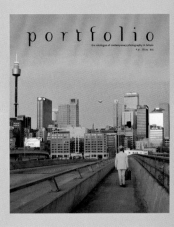

PORTFOLIO is the best way to keep informed about the most innovative photographic art created and shown in Britain. Published in June and December each year, PORTFOLIO combines the current reviews and contemporary interests of a magazine with the quality reproductions and detailed information of an exhibition catalogue.

Past issues of PORTFOLIO have featured the work of established photographic artists with in-depth essays and lively reviews from esteemed writers and curators. Back issues can be obtained individually or in a money-saving set of the ten most recent catalogues.

Issue 30
Alexa Wright
Michael Danner
Tom Hunter
Wendy McMurdo
Samantha Bell
Tom Vincent-Townend
David Wishart
Christopher Stewart
Ori Gersht
Orla Deevy
Kirsty Anderson

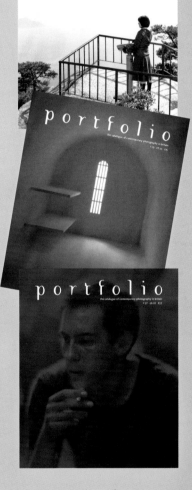

Issue 23
Helen Chadwick
Jeff Wall
Susan Hiller
Keith Piper
Orlan
Clare Strand
Liz Rideal
Katrina Lithgow
Jim Harold
Clement Cooper

Issue 25
Mat Collishaw
Catherine Yass
Karen Knorr
Hannah Collins
Evergon
Roger Palmer
Anthony Haughey
Lynn Silverman
Peter Lavery
John Darwell
Anne Bjerge Hansen

Issue 27
Paul Graham
Rineke Dikjstra
Marie-Jo Lafontaine
Joan Fontcuberta
Gabriele Basilico
Hiroshi Sugimoto
Jorma Puranen
Abigail Lane
Karen Ingham
Suky Best
Jago Brown

Issue 29
James Casebere
Andreas Gursky
Mark Power
Hannah Starkey
John Stezaker
Deborah Baker
Lesley Shearer
John Askew
Josef Koudelka
Jon Thompson
Melanie Manchot

Issue 22
Paul Graham
Allan Sekula
Joel-Peter Witkin
Martin Parr
Pavel Büchler
Helen Sear
Wendy McMurdo
Lucinda Devlin
Dorte Eisfeldt
Ann Mandelbaum

Issue 24
Calum Colvin
Gabriel Orozco
John Goto
Susan Trangmar
Willie Doherty
Richard Billingham
Robert Mapplethorpe
Jim Mooney
Annette Heyer

Issue 26
Avi Holtzman
Rut Blees Luxemburg
David Griffiths
Britta Jaschinski
Jim Harold
Bridget Smith
Owen Logan
Robin Dance
James Morris
Torsten Lauschman

Issue 28
Sharon Kivland
Sophie Calle
Joy Gregory
Jorges Molder
Yinka Shonibare
Zarina Bhimji
Tracey Moffatt
Robin Gillanders
Bryndis Snæbjörnsdóttir
Kate Mellor
Detlef Henrichs

Issue 21
Andres Serrano
Helen Chadwick
Olivier Richon
Zarina Bhimji
Catherine Yass
Roger Palmer
Andrea Fisher
Hannah Collins

Issue 20
Yve Lomax
David Williams
Thomas Joshua Cooper
Mari Mahr
David Hiscock
Lynn Silverman
Lesley Punton
Roddy Buchanan

subscriptions and back issues

UK: Individuals – £30 for 4 issues / £17 for 2 issues   Institutions, Libraries and Colleges – £45 for 4 issues / £25 for 2 issues
EUROPE – £45 for 4 issues / £25 for 2 issues   WORLDWIDE – £55 for 4 issues / £30 for 2 issues

☐ **Please start my (4 issue/2 issue)** *(please indicate)* **subscription to Portfolio with Number 32 (Dec 2000)**

☐ **Please send me back issue numbers** *(please indicate)* _____ **at £10.50 (UK) £11.50 (Europe) £14.50 (Worldwide)**

☐ **Please send me a set of ten back issues (Numbers 21 – 30) at £79 (UK) £99 (Europe) £119 (Worldwide)**

☐ **I enclose a (Sterling) cheque (made payable to PORTFOLIO) for £** _____

☐ **Or debit my Access/Visa/Mastercard** *(delete as applicable)*

Name _____   Expiry Date _____

Address _____

                                          Postcode _____

Signed _____

**Return to Portfolio, 43 Candlemaker Row, Edinburgh, EH1 2QB Scotland UK
Tel (44) 0131 220 1911 Fax (44) 0131 226 4287 Email portfolio@ednet.co.uk**

UNIVERSITY OF WESTMINSTER

School of Communication & Creative Industries

Harrow Campus Watford Road, Harrow HA1 3TP
Website www.wmin.ac.uk

The **University of Westminster** is *the* place for the critical and historical study of photographic arts, culture and sciences. Renowned for innovative courses in the theory and practice of photography, graduates go onto successful careers in the arts, advertising, media and related photographic industries.
See the student exhibitions and/or call the Admissions Office on **020 7911 5903** for application details.

Student Exhibitions

309 Regent Street, London W1 Tel 020 7911 5974
Mon-Fri 10am-8pm, Sat & Sun 10am-5pm

BA (Hons) Photographic & Digital Arts
14 – 17 June
BA (Hons) Photography & Multimedia (Part Time)
19 – 25 June
MA Photographic Studies
Year 1 29 June – 9 July, **Year 2** 1 – 17

NAPIER UNIVERSITY
EDINBURGH

PHOTOGRAPHY, FILM & TELEVISION

WORK BY STUDENTS OF THE BA (Hons)
PHOTOGRAPHY, FILM AND TV PROGRAMME

EXHIBITION

ESU, 23 Atholl Crescent, Edinburgh EH3 8HQ
Tel 0131 229 1528

Private viewing
27 June 6pm - 9pm

Public viewing
28 June - 1 July (inclusive), 11am - 8pm
(except Friday 30 June, 11am - 7pm)

FILM SHOW

Filmhouse, Lothian Road, Edinburgh
Tel 0131 228 6380
26 June, Cinema 1, 6.00 - 8.00 (invite only)

PUBLICATION: "TRACE"
64-page full colour book and CD Rom
Book: (ISBN) 0-9533274-4-2)
CD-Rom: (ISBN 0-9533274-6-9)

FELLOWSHIP IN PHOTOGRAPHY AND IMAGING

In collaboration with the Scottish Arts Council, the Department wishes to appoint a Fellow for a six month period between October 2000 and March 2001. This is the third year of this highly successful scheme and will give an artist working in the area of digital media/photography the opportunity to produce a body of creative work for exhibition and/or publication. Fee £8000 plus £1500 contribution towards materials. **Closing date Friday 23 June 2000.**

For more information about the Fellowship and details of our two new MA programmes in Visual Cultural Research Practice and European Film & Multimedia Development visit our web site on:

www.napier.ac.uk/depts/pftv/pftv/pftvframe.html

or contact: **PFTV, Napier University**
61 Marchmont Road, Edinburgh, EH9 1HU, Scotland.
Tel 0131 455 5203, Fax 0131 455 5224

NAPIER UNIVERSITY
EDINBURGH

**Investing in teaching and research
to serve the community**

---

eca
edinburgh college of art

DEGREE SHOW 2000

17 – 27 June 2000
Mon – Thur 10am – 8pm Fri Sat Sun 10am – 5pm

School of Visual Communication
Film/TV • Photography • Animation
Graphic Design • Illustration

School of Design & Applied Arts
Ceramics • Furniture • Glass & Architectural Glass
Interior Design • Jewellery & Silversmithing • Fashion
Performance Costume • Textiles

School of Drawing & Painting
Painting • Printmaking • Tapestry

School of Sculpture

School of Architecture

School of Landscape Architecture

For further information contact
Sarah O'Neill, **Edinburgh College of Art**
Lauriston Place Edinburgh
Tel 0131 221 6009 Email s.oneill@eca.ac.uk

Glasgow School of Art

School of Fine Art Degree Show

Glasgow School of Art
167 Renfrew Street Glasgow G3 6RQ tel 0141 353 4561

Private View
Friday 23 June 2000 6 - 9pm

Open to Public
Saturday 24 June - Friday 30 June 2000
Monday - Saturday 10am - 4pm Sunday 12 - 4pm

Master of Fine Art Show

CCA at McLellan Galleries
270 Sauchiehall Street Glasgow tel 0141 331 1854

Private View
Friday 23 June 2000 6-9pm

Open to Public
Saturday 24 June - Saturday 1 July 2000
Daily 10am - 6pm
Sunday 11am - 6pm

ffotogallery

Melanie Manchot
INTIMATE DISTANCE
29 April – 3 June 2000

Just Another Day
WALES AT THE TURN OF THE MILLENNIUM
10 June – 22 July 2000

Chris Steele Perkins
NOTES FROM AFGHANISTAN
29 July – 2 September 2000

The British Art Show 5
9 September – 4 November 2000

West
THE 1ST WALES FFOTOBIENNAL
11 November – 23 December 2000

Peter Finnemore
GWENDRAETH HOUSE
Available for tour

Peter Finnemore, My Head is my Only Home, 1997

FFOTOGALLERY

31 Charles Street CARDIFF CF10 2GA

Tel (029) 2034 1667 Fax (029) 2034 1672
e-mail: info@ffotogallery.freeserve.co.uk

Open Tuesday – Saturday, 10.30 – 5.30

FUNDING
by SAC

Could you or your organisation benefit from arts funding? Then we may be able to help.

At the Scottish Arts Council we provide funds, information and advice to artists and arts organisations throughout Scotland.

Through Government grants and National Lottery funding we support crafts, combined arts (arts centres, festivals etc), dance, drama, literature, music and the visual arts.

For more information visit our website or contact the SAC Help Desk team and ask for a copy of *Funds* which contains a full list of SAC's funding schemes.

The Help Desk is open between 10am - 12 noon and 2pm - 4pm, Monday to Friday.

The Scottish Arts Council,
12 Manor Place, Edinburgh EH3 7DD
Phone: 0131 240 2443 or 2444   Fax: 0131 225 9833
E-mail: help.desk@scottisharts.org.uk   Web: www.sac.org.uk

THE SCOTTISH **ARTS** COUNCIL

Our aim is to play our part in creating a dynamic arts environment which values
the artist and enhances the quality of life for the people of Scotland.

SHARON KIVLAND

le bonheur des femmes
(the scent of a woman)

Edinburgh International Festival
1 August ~ 2 September 2000 Monday ~ Saturday 10.30 ~ 5.30 Admission Free

PORTFOLIO GALLERY
43 Candlemaker Row Edinburgh EH1 2QB Tel (44) 131 220 1911 Fax (44) 131 226 4287 Email portfolio@ednet.co.uk

Carol Goodall ARPS

GET MORE OUT OF
PHOTOGRAPHY

If you'd like to improve your skills and meet other photographers, why not join the 10,000 members of the RPS worldwide? You'll receive the Photographic Journal free, be able to join regional and special interest groups, work for a renowned RPS Distinction, attend workshops and much more besides.
Call 01225 310363 (24hrs).

RPS
THE ROYAL PHOTOGRAPHIC SOCIETY

FALMOUTH
College of Arts

PgDip Photography: Critical Practice

This innovative one-year, full-time postgraduate diploma focuses on the dynamic relationship between photographic practice and theory.

The programme commences in October 2000 and offers the opportunity to:-

• undertake a self-negotiated project relating to social and cultural issues, requiring photographic content

• utilise the art of photography through a variety of forms and present it publicly in a broad range of contexts and environments

This is designed for practitioners and graduates from art and design programmes as well as from other disciplines.

Please contact Admissions for an application form.

For details of our Open Days, please contact Reception.

Falmouth College of Arts
Woodlane, Falmouth, Cornwall TR11 4RH
Telephone: 01326 211077 Fax: 01326 212261
Email: admissions@falmouth.ac.uk
Investing in Excellence in Art, Communication & Design

A University Sector College

Marzena Pogorzaly
Iceworks

PAUL RYAN

A landscape photograph connects us with the birth of the medium; a landscape photograph of Antarctica, however modern, connects us with the birth of time. Almost a century has passed since Hubert Ponting and Frank Hurley first captured Antarctica on film, but the landscape remains as bleakly elemental as it was when Scott and Shackleton ventured through it and into history. Antarctica is the last continent on Earth to remain unchanged by man. Revolutions, social, political and industrial, have passed it by. It is an eternal reminder of the wild dawn of our planet's life; a stark *memento mori* of the world's end.

The appeal of such a vast wilderness lies in the fact that it carries no history beyond the natural history of itself; there is a rare purity in this. This purity attracts scientists and adventurers, and the photographer Marzena Porgorzaly certainly has something of both these types

within her. But she is also an artist, and it is her artist's eye that allows her to render the extraordinary variety of the last wild place. A British citizen, born and raised in Poland, Pogorzaly studied marine biology and oceanography in her homeland before settling, a voluntary exile, in Britain. Edward W. Said has observed that the exile has access to at least two cultures, but Pogorzaly has extended her exile to embrace a part of the world with no indigenous human population, one that defies civilisation and has no culture at all. Where is the great music of Antarctica? Where its poetry, its painting, its sculpture? The last of these is easy to identify, for it is everywhere present in Pogorzaly's images. The elements have sculpted shapes which resemble parodies or abstractions of familiar objects. A phantom ship, fossilised beasts, an abandoned wedding cake, calcified plants and any number of imagined

correspondences with the wider world. Even the male and female genitalia are here, and how Antarctica mocks our pitifully human dimensions.

To speak of nature's artistry is to run the risk of being deemed sentimental. Let us run the risk, then, for there is a kind of epic poetry in these images, and music in the sounds that lie behind them, the creaking icebergs, the singing wind. The skies alone, in the areas above the pole that still experience a kind of night, would challenge Turner. There is a glorious paradox, too. Bleak and wintry though these landscapes seem, these are portraits of the Antarctic at the height of summer. I do not use the term 'portraits' accidentally. Pogorzaly is an exceptionally gifted portraitist whose subjects have included Isiah Berlin, Alfred Brendel and Simon Schama.

In all her work there is an edge of darkness. It might seem facile to attribute this to her Polish origins, but there is more than a grain of truth in such an observation. She views the world through a glass, darkly. It is one of the more startling qualities of *Iceworks* that she has cast a dark eye on the very heart of whiteness. The result is work that goes beyond the limitations of standard photographic landscape. Pogorzaly is interested in character, and to search out the character of a place she approaches ice formations with the same honest regard she brings to the human face. She is interested, above all, in the physical. This leads naturally to sensuality, albeit a kind which is cool and unsettling. She does not flatter, but she respects. Her human portraits are unflinching in showing what life has etched upon the sitters' faces; in the same way, she records nature's imprint on the ice.

Pogorzaly has a single advantage denied to Ponting and Hurley: access to Royal Navy helicopters attached to HMS Endurance. It gives her and us a privileged point of view on the landscape, and it frees her from the clichés of the wilderness. The iris prints on show at Cardiff's Ffotogallery have about them the quality of delicately-wrought charcoal sketches. Thus Antarctica continues to defy modernity, going against the grain of technology just as Pogorzaly goes against the grain of landscape photography. Such has been human progress in recent years that we need no longer visit Antarctica to damage its ecological health. Pogorzaly presents us with a beauty beyond civilisation, a land that we disturb at our peril. She knows that nature may yet give a truthful echo to the empty boast of Shelley's Ozymandias: "look upon my works, ye mighty, and despair."

John Riddy
John Ruskin: Praeterita

SIMON MORRISEY

Praeterita 1: The Springs of Wandel

The text opposite the image reads *The Springs of Wandel*. The black-and-white photograph has a distinctive patina, a silvered tonality, and shows a steamer moored in the Thames. For a moment, the boat almost persuades you that this is not a contemporary image, but then the vinyl banner draped on its side, advertising function suites and nightclub for hire, allows the image to unfold into the present, the Millennium Eye in the process of being erected in the background.

It is perhaps not coincidental that this image features two different symbols of the evolution of the modern Labour movement – the ex-GLC headquarters County Hall and Millbank Tower, the home of the New Labour party machine – within its horizon, when the image is located as the first in a new sequential work of 28 images that the British artist John Riddy has made in response to John Ruskin's autobiography, *Praeterita*, on the centenary of his death. Known predominantly as an artist and critic, the prolific Victorian was also a political and social visionary whose thinking, which although little known today, laid the foundation for the modern Labour movement.

Praeterita 8: Vester, Camenae

Perhaps one of the most distinctive in British contemporary photography, John Riddy's practice exists in a singular relationship to a particular photographic inheritance that many would consider, like Ruskin's influence, to be eroded to the point of non-existence at the beginning of the 21st century. Riddy's black-and-white images are in some ways articles of belief in the possibilities of photography, positioned as transparent condensers for the subjects they capture. They are meditations on the particularity and poetry of place, which convey the layering and compression of space and time that surrounds us with an almost sculptural physicality and a lucidity belied by their transparency, but which is in fact due directly to it.

As Riddy began to explore Ruskin's writing in some depth for the commission, he discovered an affinity between his preoccupations and that of Ruskin that is at the heart of *Praeterita's* structure. Riddy has not illustrated the narrative of the autobiography but has rather paralleled the acts of travelling, stopping, looking and describing that preoccupied Ruskin with the same structure that lies at the

Praeterita 9: The Col de la Faucille

Praeterita 15: Cumae

Praeterita 17: The Simplon

Praeterita 6: Schaffhausen and Milan

centre of his own practice. Continuing this mirroring, Riddy views the book of his images to be the primary realisation of the work rather than the exhibition that will accompany it, positioning his own *Praeterita* in the same artistic space as Ruskin's. Each of Riddy's images in the series relates directly to a chapter of Ruskin's autobiography and is reproduced on the right hand page, opposite the title of the corresponding chapter. Set adrift from the narrative of the autobiography, Ruskin's titles form a collage of allusion that weaves a web from the familial to the mythic, the geographical to the classical, the political to the affectionate. In juxtaposition, Riddy's photographs create a sense of a fluid ebb in space and time, of moments and spaces from the past coexisting with the present. This atmosphere is often discernible in Riddy's work but here has a particular relationship to the way that time's normally accepted boundaries dissolve and become confused in Ruskin's autobiography, much of which was written in between bouts of mental illness.

Sometimes Riddy's images are a visual reference to what he believes to be the absolute hub of Ruskin's existence at that time, such as the encounter with the abbey at San Riquier in *The Col de la Faucille*, which was the first time Ruskin placed his appreciation of architecture within its social context. On other occasions, they are incidental moments, a space fleetingly described by the writer that has a resonance outside of his own narrative. In many, Riddy has excluded reference to the contemporary world, allowing the spaces depicted to exist in a flux between past and present, an unspecific time. When it makes itself felt, the present is mostly quietly implied through subtle details – a rack of tourist leaflets in a hotel lobby, the vinyl banner on the steamer. Rarely, Riddy allows his awareness of the compression of co-existing times to manifest itself with a violent beauty. *Rome* depicts the monumental architecture of the city's classical past engulfed in the morass of the contemporary cityscape, Riddy creating a poetry of collision that was laced through the body of work he recently completed whilst the Sargeant Fellow at the British School at Rome in 1998/9.

But even these moments of intense implosion occur within an expansive, spatial silence that the artist creates with the levelling stillness of his lens. This atmosphere also envelopes the different micro-climates present in the series. The images taken in Britain, for example, are predominantly matter-of-fact, solidly rooted in their site. The wooden park gazebo in *Vester, Camenae*, veers towards the prosaic, its municipal litter bin and ▶

Praeterita 14: Rome

Praeterita 16: Fontainebleau

Praeterita 25: The Grand Chartreuse

crazy-pathed paths a counterpoint to the pastoral Herne Hill of Ruskin's childhood. However, the European sites, frequently classic stops on The Grand Tour, such as *Fontainebleau*, have a more Romantic quality. It is the reoccurring images of the Alps that are most elusive; *The Simplon* appears like a solidifying vision, symbolising in its austere grandeur the loci of Ruskin's Romantic inspiration. Mount Blanc in particular haunts the series. Riddy shuffles Ruskin's allusions to the place with his own, introducing a dislocated space between them. In *The Grande Chartreuse*, Riddy presents us with a hotel lobby, but it is unspecified whether this is the contemporary interior of Ruskin's haunt L'Hotel Du Mont Blanc. As in Riddy's earlier image *Soule*, 1996, which depicts the interior of a small cafe in the Pyrenees dominated by a mural of the exterior landscape, the interior in *The Grande Chartreuse* is not the subject itself but a pictorial structure, a space redefined as a frame for the represented exterior in the painting of the Alps that hangs on the wall.

The image that actually bears the name of *L'Hotel Du Mont Blanc* does not depict the establishment. Riddy's image shows a fragment of a rather ordinary village in the Swiss Alps – a clutch of scrappy, nondescript buildings and some scrubby grass interlaced with trees. Two equally scrappy, nondescript small cars are parked at right angles in the centre of the image. The totemic presence of the mountain is written over the scene, but only faintly, its form almost bleeding into the white of Riddy's sky. The image is strangely reminiscent of so many pictures of deserted villages we have been exposed to over the duration of the Balkan conflict. Some other Europe, where the majesty of landscape sits in equal coexistence with a hard fought existence and an inheritance that, if you are lucky, consists of some scrubby grass and a nondescript second-hand car. The image is perhaps one of the most important in the series, its rather disheartening atmosphere seeming to make a form of mute comment on our communal inability to fulfil Ruskin's social and political vision.

Ruskin's *Praeterita* and Riddy's own practice are in their own ways autobiographies in the form of travelogues – a belief that it is in temporarily leaving behind the place where you are from and attempting to describe the place in which you have arrived that we come to understand what place we have in the world. On their mirrored journeys both artists found themselves standing at the site of the battle of Waterloo outside Brussels, which Ruskin had visited on his travels in Europe and to which Riddy followed to create the image *Schaffhausen and Milan*. If time was to compress at that spot Ruskin and Riddy would share their view over the mist covered fields with the contemporary German writer W.G Sebald. Perhaps it is more than coincidence that these three would intersect here and that Sebald too should share Ruskin and Riddy's deep involvement with place as the catalyst for reflection. Sebald recounts his visit to Waterloo in his hypnotic *The Rings of Saturn*. Ostensibly, the book is a travelogue, underpinned with the structure of a walk across the distinctive landscape of Suffolk. But Sebald's narrative is more an extended essay on the mutability of human existence within the complexities of time than any conventional understanding of fiction; fluidly looping and wheeling between recollection and experience, melting between different times and spaces – often separated by entire centuries and continents – and linked together more by the associative processes of the landscape of the author's life and knowledge than by any reference to the English countryside within which he walked.

In some ways Riddy's practice is the visual accompaniment to Sebald's prose. The diversity of geographical and historical moments which the artist captures are woven together perhaps more by his act of describing them with the camera than by their inherent qualities. Riddy's images are suffuse with a stillness that is the condensation of his contemplation of our limitations within the greater actions of time, which parallels Sebald's own attempt to illustrate the transience of the individual within history. It is a position with which Ruskin would have held more than a little sympathy.

Praeterita is organised by The Laboratory at the Ruskin School of Drawing and Fine Art, University of Oxford, as part of the programme of events to mark the centenary of the death of John Ruskin in 2000. A fully illustrated publication is available at £20 (ISBN 0 9538525 0 4) telephone 01865 276940.

Peter Finnemore
A Sense of Place

MARK DURDEN

My Head is My Only Home, 1997

Peter Finnemore makes photographs about his home place in the Welsh-speaking heartland of rural west Wales, where his family have lived for five generations. Many of his photographs in his home, Gwendraeth House, are centred upon objects and possessions: human presence is implied through association, in particular through the felt sense of contiguity between belongings and their (absent) owners.

When Finnemore occasionally makes a portrait, the relationship set up between the sitter and his or her possessions is important. In the tender portrait of his grandmother, *Better Rooms*, the elderly woman sits in a rocking chair facing the viewer. She is holding a comb by which she has just made herself ready to be photographed. One is struck by the picture's rich formal interplay of different patterns: the web-like pattern of the crocheted shawl on his grandmother's lap set against the floral-patterned garments displayed behind her, which are in turn played off against the ferns on the wallpaper. The Zimmer frame and walking sticks arranged by her side suggest her present difficulty with walking, while the array of dresses behind suggest her youthful past. The heart form which the sticks make on the Zimmer frame – right at

Wallpaper Fragrance, 1996

Threshold II, 1998

the centre of this image – is not fortuitous, but a subtle reiteration of the photographer's loving and caring view of the person depicted. Sentiment is integral to this photograph. The heart shape recurs in the sticks which lie across the carpet in another picture which show a woman's slippers and shoes, some more worn and used than others, all sorted and carefully laid out in rows on the floral carpet. It is a simple, eloquent and moving photograph, which speaks of our relationship to the belongings of someone who has died, our attempt to order and sort things, ordinary objects which become special and meaningful because of the associations and memories they bring of the person who once wore them.

In *Wallpaper Fragrance*, a cast shadow leaves the profile of a face over fern-patterned wallpaper. The title calls attention to the way in which the shadow face appears to be smelling one of the ferns on the wallpaper. The ephemeral shadow portrait is the artist's father, and calls up the story of the mythic origins of the art of painting in which a Corinthian maid drew in outline on a wall the shadow of her beloved's face. Fixing his shadow would remind her of the face of the lover who was leaving to go to war and exorcise the danger he was in. The profile in shadow in Finnemore's picture appears to face an open door. Is he too about to leave?

When Finnemore moves outside to the garden to make photographs, his pictures change. If the interior pictures are marked by a certain privacy and intimacy, then the photographs he makes in the garden of his home are preoccupied with more universal symbols and archetypes. In many of these photographs, plants, flowers and animals symbolise a life force, a pantheistic joy in life. Natural cycles, the changes of seasons, of growth, decay and rebirth, are integral to this work. When Finnemore makes and photographs human shapes in the ground, associations of burial and death are offset by the sense of new life and regeneration connoted by the sunflower seeds, used to outline the human form on the soil in *Divination*. For *The Green Man*, the artist carefully tended and grew plants in the shape of a human figure on the ground, a symbol of fertility, of new life and growth after death.

The sunflower is an important symbol for Finnemore, signifying a radiant centre and a life-force, linked up with other central and centred forms: in particular the little rickety wooden house – made from an old door from Gwendraeth House – which crops up in a number of photographs. *My Head is My Only Home* shows the artist surrounded and dwarfed by sunflowers with the miniature

house held above his head. Such images are for Finnemore very much "about the search for homes, a central root point of security." The photograph showing the little wooden house going up in flames, *Screaming House*, thus serves as a particularly painful image, becoming legible in terms of losing a sense of place, belonging, home.

Lesson 56-Wales consists of a series of colour photographs of pages from old school books – his grandmother's – published at the height of the British Empire. The work was undertaken in the months following the Welsh Assembly vote on 18 September 1997. In these pictures personal family history is played out against a history of colonial rule and imposition. The handwritten name and address of his grandmother, Venus Aneira Bowen, provides a subjective counterpart to the formality and authority of the language and illustrations in the school books. Doodles of crowns which recur among the pages – additions by the artist? – reiterate the books' imperialism.

His grandmother's signature and address is linked to an assertion of identity and home. Its preservation is important as a link with the past, a sign of Welsh identity, however fragile, among these books with their Anglo-centric versions of history. One colour photograph in the series shows a letter bearing the name and address of the artist's grandmother, placed on a shelf against stacks of books about Wales, recent and old, in English and Welsh. Like this letter, much of Peter Finnemore's work centres on this woman. She is integral to his attachment to his home place. The pathos and tenderness of so many of his pictures stems from this loving relationship. And as the photographs of her school books make clear, this relationship is caught up with Finnemore's own feelings about his own culture, his own sense of national identity.

The recent founding of the Welsh Assembly signals a reassertion of identity, which Finnemore senses is now taking place at grass roots level, within a wider shift of feeling towards cultural consciousness and national perception in his country. Much as melancholy and loss characterise his pictures, they are not simply reducible to a narrative of loss, in terms of nation. The sentiment and feeling of this work is caught up with hopes of change: the love and care underlying many of his interior pictures and portraits, the symbols of life-forces and regeneration in the garden photographs, and now in these pictures of old books, which also make visible the fragility and contradictions involved in feelings of belonging, of home.

This is an edited version of the essay 'Wearing In' commissoned for Peter Finnemore's exhibition catalogue, *Gwendraeth House*, published by Ffotogallery, Cardiff.

Screaming House, 1997

Contributors

Artists

Elisa Sighicelli
Partially backlit lightboxes
Courtesy Laure Genillard Gallery, London
Elisa Sighicelli is an artist based in London. Her work was exhibited in Residual Property at Portfolio Gallery, Edinburgh, in March 2000 and at the Centro Galego de Arte Contemporanea, Santigo de Compostela in March 2000 and in *Is there anyone home?* at Gallery Westland Place, London, 18 May - 24 June 2000.

Miriam Bäckström
Cibachrome prints on aluminium
Courtesy Nils Stærk, Copenhagen
Miriam Bäckström is an artist based in Stockholm. Her work was shown at the Institute of Contemporary Arts in London, in January - February 2000. She is represented by Nils Stærk in Copenhagen.

Luisa Lambri
Cibachrome prints
Courtesy Studio Guenzani, Milan
Luisa Lambri is an artist based in Milan. Her work has recently been shown at the 48 Biennale Internazionale d'Arte, Venezia. She is currently exhibition at Fotogalleriet in Oslo and at Gallery Koyanagi in Tokyo, and will have a one-person show at Kettle's Yard, Cambridge, in September 2000.

Anne Zahalka
Leisureland Series, C-type prints
Fortresses and Frontiers Series, Duratran Lightboxes
Anne Zahalka is an artist based in Sydney, who lectures at Sydney University. Her series *Fortresses and Frontiers* was shown in the exhibition *Journeys in the Dreamland*, at Ffotogallery, Cardiff, 29 January - 22 March 2000, and subsequently at Robert Sandelson Gallery in London. A catalogue for the exhibition *Journeys in the Dreamland* (ISBN 1 872771 65 3) is available from Ffotogallery (01222 341667).

Sharon Kivland
C-type prints on aluminium
Sharon Kivland is an artist, writer and curator. She is an associate Senior Lecturer at Sheffield Hallam University and is a Research Associate of the Centre for Freudian Analysis and Research, London. Her exhibition *le bonheur des femmes* will be shown at Portfolio Gallery, Edinburgh, during the Edinburgh International Festival, 1 August - 2 September 2000, at Galerie Vu, Quebec, September 2000 La Centrale Gallery (Powerhouse), Montreal, September 2000 and Le Tirangle, Rennes, March 2001. She is represented by Wigmore Fine Arts.

David Williams
C-type photographs mounted on aluminium
David Williams is an artist based in Edinburgh and is Head of Photography at Edinburgh College of Art. His series *Stillness and Occurrence* will be shown at Zelda Cheatle Gallery in London in September 2000.

Sam Taylor-Wood
C-type colour prints (framed)
Courtesy Jay Jopling (London)
Sam Taylor-Wood is an artist based in London and is represented by White Cube Gallery. The Soliloquy series is reproduced in a catalogue of her work published to coincide with her exhibition at the Fondazione Prada, Madrid, in 1999.

Paul Seawright
C-type prints on aluminium
Paul Seawright is Head of the Centre for Photographic Research at the University of Wales College, Newport. His work was shown at Interim Art 3 February - 5 March 2000 and is currently shown within the British Art Show 5.

Patricia Macdonald
The play grounds series, no. 6: burnt moorland, grouse shooting
24-part work, each 53 x 35.7 cm, Ilfochrome prints
Patricia Macdonald is an Edinburgh-based artist and writer. She has recently exhibited at the Museet for Fotokunst, Denmark, the Ingleby Gallery, Edinburgh and Art 99, with forthcoming exhibitions at The National Museums of Scotland, the Talbot Rice Gallery, Edinburgh, and the Architectural Association, London. Her most recent book is: *Once in Europa*, John Berger and Patricia Macdonald, Bloomsbury, London, 1999 (ISBN 0 7475 4449 2) price £20.

Garry Fabian Miller
Dia Destruction Prints. **Courtesy PhotoWorks**
Garry Fabian Miller was Artist in Residence at Petworth House An exhibition of the work was held at Petworth House, West Sussex, in September 1999. A book *Tracing Light: Art and Culture at Petworth* 1820-2000 by David Alan mellor will be published by PhotoWorks in late 2000 (01622 621 134)

Jem Southam
C-type photographs. **Courtesy PhotoWorks**
Jem Southam lectures in Design Photography at Exeter School of Art and Design, University of Plymouth. His exhibition, *The Shape of Time*, was shown at Towner Art Gallery in association with PhotoWorks 31 March - 4 June 2000. A book of the same title will be published by PhotoWorks in association with Cornerhouse.

Susanne Ramsenthaler
C-type photographs
Susanne Ramsenthaler is an artist based in Edinburgh and lectures in photography at Edinburgh College of Art. Her work will be shown in Point Gallery, Omaha, Nebraska during May - June 2000 and at Stroud House Gallery, Stroud, Gloucestershire, 6 May - 3 June 2000.

Keren Amiran
28 C-type prints each 42 x 31 cm
Keren Amiran is an Israeli artist based in London. Her work was shown at the Heinrich Böll Foundation, Tel Aviv, in February 1999, the Cubitt Gallery, London in March 2000, and the Centre for Contemporary Culture in Barcelona in April 2000

Marzena Pogorzaly
Iris Prints
Marzena Pogorzaly is a marine biologist and oceanographer who trained at the University of Gdnask before relocating to London to pursue her career as a freelance photographer. The exhibition *Iceworks* was shown at Ffotogallery in Cardiff in September 1999. Marzena Pogorzaly would like to thank the Captain and crew of HMS Endurance and the Government of the British Antarctic Territory, without whose help this project would not have been possible.

John Riddy
Silver gelatin prints, 10 x 8 inches
Courtesy Frith Street Gallery, London
John Riddy was commissioned by The Laboratory at the Ruskin School of Drawing and Fine Art, University of Oxford, to produce a series of photographs suggested by *Praeterita* the autobiography of John Ruskin. The exhibition begins a tour at The Ruskin Gallery, Sheffield, 3 June - 15 July 2000. A fully illustrated publication is available price £20 (ISBN 0 9538525 0 4) from Ruskin School of Drawing and Fine Art (01865 276940).

Peter Finnemore
Black and white, selenium-toned, silver gelatin prints. **Courtesy Ffotogallery, Cardiff**
Peter Finnemore is an artist based in Llanelli, Wales. His exhibition *Gwendraeth House* was shown at Ffotogallery, Cardiff from 18 March - 22 April 2000. The catalogue of the exhibition, with essay by Mark Durden (ISBN 1 872771 70) is available from Ffotogallery (01222 341667).

Writers

Roy Exley is a freelance writer, art critic and curator who writes regularly for Contemporary Visual Art, Creative Camera and Untitled.

Pavel Büchler is an artist and is Research Professor of Art and Design at Manchester Metropolitan University.

Jane Rendell is an architectural historian and theorist and Lecturer in Architecture in the University of Nottingham.

Susanna Beaumont is Art Editor of *The List* Magazine and a writer based in Edinburgh.

Mark Durden is an artist and Senior Lecturer in the History and Theory of Photography at the University of Derby.

James Lawson is a teacher at Edinburgh University.

David Alan Mellor is an independent curator, writer, and Professor of History of Art at Sussex University.

David Chandler is a writer, curator and Director of PhotoWorks.

Stella Santacatterina is a curator, writer and freelance lecturer based in London.

Paul Ryan is a writer and lecturer based in London.

Simon Morrissey is a critic and independent curator based in London.